Landlords and Rogues

In and Around York's
Old Inns

To Ryan and Kelly,

A little something to remind
you of York

Love Louis and Aimee

xxx

FOUL DEEDS AND SUSPICIOUS DEATHS Series

Wharncliffe's *Foul Deeds and Suspicious Deaths* series explores, in detail, crimes of passion, brutal murders and foul misdemeanours from early modern times to the present day. Victorian street crime, mysterious deaths and modern murders tell tales where passion, jealousy and social deprivation brought unexpected violence to those involved. From unexplained death and suicide to murder and manslaughter, the books provide a fascinating insight into the lives of both victims and perpetrators as well as society as a whole.

Other titles in the series include:

Foul Deeds and Suspicious Deaths in Birmingham, Nick Billingham
ISBN: 1-903425-96-4. £10.99

Foul Deeds and Suspicious Deaths in Bolton, Glynis Cooper
ISBN: 1-903425-63-8. £9.99

Foul Deeds and Suspicious Deaths in Colchester, Patrick Denney
ISBN: 1-903425-80-8. £10.99

Foul Deeds and Suspicious Deaths in Coventry, David McGrory
ISBN: 1-903425-57-3. £9.99

Foul Deeds and Suspicious Deaths Around Derby, Kevin Turton
ISBN: 1-903425-76-X. £9.99

Foul Deeds and Suspicious Deaths in & around Durham, Maureen Anderson
ISBN: 1-903425-46-8. £9.99

Foul Deeds and Suspicious Deaths in Hampstead, Holburn & St Pancras, Mark Aston
ISBN: 1-903425-94-8. £10.99

Foul Deeds and Suspicious Deaths in Hull, David Goodman
ISBN: 1-903425-43-3. £9.99

Foul Deeds and Suspicious Deaths Around Leicester, Kevin Turton
ISBN: 1-903425-73-1. £10.99

Foul Deeds and Suspicious Deaths in London's East End, Geoffrey Howse
ISBN: 1-903425-71-9. £10.99

Foul Deeds and Suspicious Deaths in London's West End, Geoffrey Howse
ISBN: 1-845630-01-7. £10.99

Foul Deeds and Suspicious Deaths in Manchester, Martin Baggoley
ISBN: 1-903425-65-4. £9.99

Foul Deeds and Suspicious Deaths in Newcastle, Maureen Anderson
ISBN: 1-903425-34-4. £9.99

Foul Deeds and Suspicious Deaths Around Newport, Terry Underwood
ISBN: 1-903425-59-X. £9.99

Foul Deeds and Suspicious Deaths in and Around Scunthorpe, Stephen Wade
ISBN: 1-903425-88-3. £9.99

Foul Deeds and Suspicious Deaths in Stratford & S. Warwickshire, Nick Billingham
ISBN: 1-903425-99-9. £10.99

More Foul Deeds and Suspicious Deaths in Wakefield, Kate Taylor
ISBN: 1-903425-48-4. £9.99

Foul Deeds and Suspicious Deaths in York, Keith Henson
ISBN: 1-903425-33-6. £9.99

Foul Deeds and Suspicious Deaths on the Yorkshire Coast, Alan Whitworth
ISBN: 1-903425-01-8. £9.99

Please contact us via any of the methods below for more information or a catalogue.

WHARNCLIFFE BOOKS
47 Church Street – Barnsley – South Yorkshire S70 2AS
Tel: 01226 734555 – 734222; Fax: 01226 724438
E-mail: enquiries@pen-and-sword.co.uk
Website: www.wharncliffebooks.co.uk

Landlords and Rogues

In and Around York's Old Inns

PETE COXON

Illustrated by David Questa

Series Editor
Brian Elliott

Wharncliffe Books

First Published in Great Britain in 2006 by
Wharncliffe Books
an imprint of
Pen and Sword Books Ltd
47 Church Street
Barnsley
South Yorkshire
S70 2AS

Copyright © Pete Coxon and David Questa 2006

ISBN: 1 845630 16 5

Typeset in 10/12pt Plantin by Concept, Huddersfield.

Printed and bound in England by
Biddles Ltd.

Pen and Sword Books Ltd incorporates the Imprints of
Pen & Sword Aviation, Pen & Sword Maritime,
Pen & Sword Military, Wharncliffe Books,
Pen & Sword Select, Pen and Sword Military Classics
and Leo Cooper.

For a complete list of Pen & Sword titles please contact
PEN & SWORD BOOKS LIMITED
47 Church Street
Barnsley
South Yorkshire
S70 2AS
England
E-mail: enquiries@pen-and-sword.co.uk
Website: www.pen-and-sword.co.uk

Contents

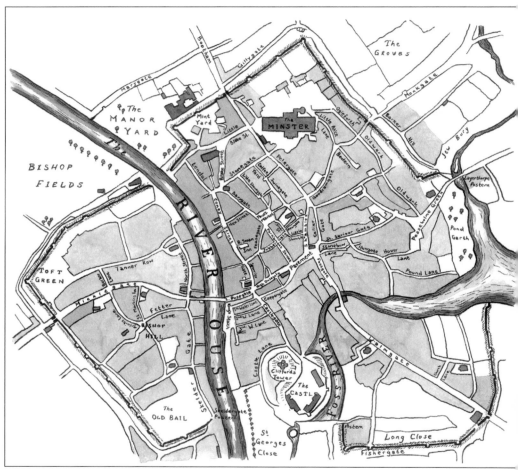

Nineteenth century York

Introduction

A young Italian at the *Whale Fishery*
1857

Joseph Antonio fastened his fashionable necktie around the collar of his dress shirt and eased on his black kid gloves. Having once been a soldier in the Italian Legion, the young Piedmontese liked to look his best. On the table in his room, he carefully placed a piece of paper on which was drawn a heart pierced with an arrow, and a picture of himself and a young lady. Upon her partly obliterated likeness he gently placed a lock of her hair. Next to these he placed a letter addressed to his father, saying that he had resolved to destroy himself on account of the treachery of a friend in York. Having completed his preparations, he placed a washbasin under his arm, opened his vein with a razor and watched the blood flow.

It was 10 o'clock on the morning of Sunday 4 January, and Joseph had not worked since before Christmas. Another young Italian was now making his way to Joseph's lonely room at the *Whale Fishery* public house and there he found the basin almost filled with blood and his friend unconscious and close to death. He raised the alarm and two surgeons were called, Mr Allen from nearby St Saviourgate and Mr Hanbury, house surgeon at the hospital. They administered

He watched the blood flow

stimulants to Joseph and managed to stop the bleeding just in time to save his life. It was reported that by the Wednesday night he had recovered well enough to be returned to the workhouse.[1]

The *Whale Fishery* was a typical mid-nineteenth century town inn, small and frugal by today's standards. Its only drinking area was a smoke room which was also the family's living room. Toilet facilities consisted of a single water closet which the family and customers had to share and a urinal, both in a yard open to the street.

The inn was kept by fifty-nine-year-old landlord Christopher Bean who had been a harpooner in the Polar seas in his younger days. After leaving the sea he had moved to the city and opened his first inn close to the fish market, naming it the *Carrier's Arms* after a relative's transport business next door. In 1836 he moved to his new inn in Hungate and named it after the happy hunting grounds of his youth.

York's population in 1800 was just short of 17,000. Halfway between London and Edinburgh, it was a major stopping place in the great coaching era, with more than sixty coaches speeding daily across the old Ouse Bridge, lined with ancient timber-framed houses, and through the narrow crowded streets.

By the middle of the century the coaching days were over and the city was becoming a major railway centre. The old coaching inns faded away, replaced by new buildings to the south of the river such as the *North Eastern*, *Great Northern*, and *Railway Hotels*.

Farmers walked or rode into the city, bringing their produce and livestock to the markets and fairs, and stayed in the inns surrounding the market places such as the *Woolpack*, the *Drovers Inn* and the *Spotted Cow* which had stabling for twenty-seven horses and sheds for sixty head of cattle.

The cavalry barracks had been built at the end of the eighteenth century, freeing space in the inns and stables, but for most of the nineteenth century infantry-men were billeted at the inns, bringing income and their fair share of trouble to the innkeepers. *The Light Horseman, Barrack Tavern* and *Rifleman* bore witness to the military presence. Other inns

Sheds for sixty head of cattle

such as *The Keel*, *The Ship*, and *The Fortunate Tar* drew custom from the river trade.

The Irish famines of the 1840s saw an influx of families looking for food and work, taking shelter in the poorer quarters, forming their own communities and frequenting pubs in the Walmgate area such as the *Sons of Erin* and the *Hibernia Tavern*.

The city was a kaleidoscope of lifestyles for which its multitude of inns was a catalyst. Here in the nineteenth century we shall meet them

Bringing their produce to the markets

all – the families who lived in the inns and their servants, the coach travellers, and strange and curious visitors who earned their living in freak shows. We shall meet soldiers and sailors, tradesmen and farmers, gourmets and gamblers, entertainers, confidence tricksters, prostitutes and thieves. In spite of heavy punishments meted out by the courts, nineteenth-century crime was rife and the city was a dangerous place.

CHAPTER 1

Crime and Punishment

Villains at the *Black Horse*
1808

On Wednesday 10 February two smart-looking men slept for the night in a room in the *Bay Horse*, Tadcaster, better-known locally as the *Slip Inn*. Josiah Wilmot and William Kitchen had the appearance of genteel travellers and were well known to the landlord John Smith, having stayed at the inn several times since the previous September. Thursday was the day of the Fair in York. Before leaving, the two men ordered their room for the following night and said they would sleep there, and at about 11 o'clock in the morning they set off without any baggage on the eight-mile journey to York, Josiah Wilmot on foot and William Kitchen on a grey Galloway pony.

In York, in the street named Pavement, stood the *Black Horse*, an inn used by drovers and market traders. Until the previous year it had been kept by John Underwood, but since he had died of consumption at the age of forty-five his widow Ann had been left to run the inn with some help from her brother, a Mr Brown. Kitchen and Wilmot arrived here in the early evening and dined with several other men. They left after their meal, but half an hour later they returned and went into the front parlour where tailor Joseph Hepworth had laid out a large amount of his cloth for sale. Wilmot felt the cloth and remarked to his companion on its fine quality. They asked Mrs Underwood for some wine and water, and stayed another hour. Kitchen came back into the inn at about 8.30 to ask the landlady what time supper would be served, but she did not see him again that night.

At 1 o'clock in the morning Mrs Underwood and her brother checked that no-one else was in the house, then locked and bolted the front and back doors and checked that the back windows in the kitchen were closed. Mrs Underwood then went upstairs to bed, followed closely by her brother.

Moses Herbert was employed as the inn's ostler, taking care of the customers' horses, and had been in the stables at 6 o'clock that evening. He had checked that the only two horses left there belonged to neighbours, then used a lock and chain to secure the door which led into the lane to Lady Peckitt's Yard behind the inn. He fastened the hayloft window before leaving the stable, his work finished for the day.

At 4.30 on the Friday morning William Turnbull, the ostler at the *Bay Horse* in Tadcaster, was already going about his duties. He saw Wilmot and Kitchen arriving back from York on foot, with a large sack loaded on the grey pony's back, and watched them put the pony inside the stable. It had been snowing heavily and when John Smith came downstairs at 5 o'clock he found the two men drying themselves by the kitchen fire after their exhausting journey.

At daylight they brought their sack out of the stable and took it up to their room. They stayed there two or three hours and came back down with their goods wrapped into two parcels. John Smith and his ostler put the parcels in a cart and the ostler took them to Mr Hartley's wagon warehouse in Tadcaster.

On the Friday morning at the *Black Horse*, chambermaid Mary Pickering was the first to come downstairs. She found the back window, the bar door and the front door all open and called Mrs Underwood. The landlady came down and found that the lock on the door to the bar had been picked. A silver pint mug, ten silver spoons and five or six gallons of brandy were missing, along with about 5*s* worth of copper coins.

Later that morning Joseph Hepworth heard of the robbery and discovered that his cloth had also been taken, a total of 150 yards, worth about £50. He followed Moses Herbert into the stables. They found the window still fastened on the inside, but the lock on the door had been picked and the chain let down. The thieves had escaped the way they came in, fastening the stable door on the outside as they left.

He saw them arriving back from York

All that remained of their haul was a silver-plated pint mug lying in the straw. A list was made of all that had been stolen and it was given to the police.

The following Monday a man called John Kirkman came into William Stephenson's tailor's shop in Spurriergate, not far from Pavement, carrying a large bundle of cloth. He gave the tailor 10½ yards for two greatcoats, 2 yards of turpentine cloth for a common coat and nearly 4 yards of patent cord for two pairs of trousers. The next day he brought Josiah Wilmot into the shop and the tailor measured him for a coat, a greatcoat and a pair of breeches. When they were ready, the clothes were sent by stagecoach to Wilmot in Leeds.

The police were now on their trail. Mrs Underwood remembered seeing Kirkman drinking a glass of ale in the *Black Horse* when the suspects had called, but at the time she had thought he was alone. It took only a few days for the police to track them down. Constable Shaw visited *The George*, an old coaching inn in Westgate, Wakefield, and found Kirkman and Wilmot there. The landlord had told him the men were carrying luggage but when the constable asked to see it Wilmot said 'No, we have no parcel at all'. It was only when the servant brought the parcels that he admitted 'They are ours jointly'.

The Guildhall

The constable arrested both men and they were put in prison to await trial. Soon afterwards they were joined by Kitchen and a man called Sam Hall who was accused of receiving the cloth knowing it to be stolen.

On Saturday 12 March they were tried at the Guildhall. The trial was very thorough and many witnesses were called. In addition to the households of the inns in York and Tadcaster, there was William Myers who appeared on behalf of William Stephenson his uncle, carrier Bernard Hobkirk, tailor Joseph Robinson of Tadcaster, William Littlewood, who identified the bottle-green cloth he had sold to Joseph Hepworth, and John Shaw, deputy constable of Wakefield. Sam Hall was acquitted but the other three prisoners were found guilty and sentenced to death. These were the only death sentences passed that day at the Guildhall, but there were thirteen more at the Castle – four for highway robbery, two for rape, two for burglary, two for horse stealing, one for forgery, one for sheep stealing and one for the theft of two Scotch cows.[1]

A sentence of death
1822

In April 1822, fifty-nine-year-old Hannah Robson was charged with the theft of a linen table cloth and some other articles from Mr Ruddock's *Old White Swan* in Goodramgate and sentenced to two months' hard labour. The pre-

He forced a shutter off one of the windows

vious month nineteen-year-old Mary Daniels had been less fortunate. She had stolen £5 from her master, John Harker, a plumber and glazier, whose business was two doors away from the *Pack Horse* near Ouse Bridge. The court at the Guildhall sentenced her to death.

That same year, on a Thursday night in November, a thief forced a shutter off one of the windows of the *Bird in Hand* at Bootham Bar. The landlady, Mrs Driffield, reported a number of items stolen, including 5s, nine silver teaspoons, six dozen plated spoons and a quantity of clothing. George

The Bird in Hand, *demolished in 1835*

Wells was later found guilty of the crime and in the May of the following year it was ordered that he should be taken from prison to one of the hulks at Chatham or Portsmouth to await deportation.[2]

A broken spoon
1829

At about noon on Saturday 28 February fourteen-year-old William White took a beefsteak into the *Coach & Horses*, Jubbergate. He asked to be allowed to cook it and was served with salt, pepper and mustard. During the afternoon it was noticed that a silver teaspoon was missing from the mustard pot. William had stolen it and later that day had given it to a younger boy, named Trainer, to sell, but he was unable to dispose of it and gave it back to William.

That evening his friend George Mitchell, also aged fourteen, took the spoon, now broken in two, to Mr Newbold's in Colliergate and offered it for sale saying he had found it in some manure. The following morning he offered it for sale in Mr Watson's shop in Low Ousegate and by this time it had been broken into three pieces. The shop assistant, aware of the robbery, detained the boy and sent for a policeman.

In court, George Mitchell told the Lord Mayor that William White had given him the spoon. Both boys were found guilty and sentenced to be transported for seven years.[3]

A man in black
1838

One Monday in June, an eighteen-year-old chimney sweep, was drinking at the *Frog Hall Tavern* in Layerthorpe. His name was John Williams, alias John Andrews. He and a number of other men continued to drink steadily through the small hours and at about 3 o'clock in the morning one of the company, a local bricklayer called William Drury, went out to the privy where one of his companions found him asleep almost two hours later. They noticed that their friend's silk handkerchief was missing and at once suspected the man in black who had hurriedly left the *Frog Hall*. They followed the sweep as far as Walmgate, where they managed to catch him and hand him over to the police. The handkerchief was found wrapped around his chest and later that day he was sent to the House of Correction to await trial. Three weeks later he was sentenced to be transported for seven years.[4]

Fourteen days for a loafer
1899

By the end of the century sentences were much more lenient. At 10.30 on an April morning, a local youth named Christopher Sullivan went into the *Bay Horse* in Monkgate. While he was drinking his pint of beer he began to insult the other customers and was ordered out. At 11 o'clock he came back in and was ordered to leave; he tried again three more times that afternoon but was turned out each time. When Mr Arnott the ostler was closing the gates, Sullivan came up to him and hit him in the face and stomach. He continued the assault, rushing at the ostler and knocking him over knelt on his chest, hitting him in the face and then kicked him on the head.

The Bay Horse, *re-named the* Keystones *in 1995*

In the police court the youth said he was employed at the brick works and earned 15*s* a week but the constable who had arrested him called him a 'loafer'. He was sentenced to fourteen days.[5]

CHAPTER 2

Tricks of the Trade

A gallon of brandy
1800

In January of the year 1800 two women walked into Mr Marmaduke Weaver's wine and spirits shop. One of them, Margaret Ryan, otherwise known as Margaret Dann, asked Mr Weaver if she could taste his brandy before buying a gallon. When he poured her a taste she told him it was so good that she would have three gallons. She produced a bladder for him to fill with a gallon of it and turning to the other woman, who seemed to be her servant, she asked her to go and fetch two more bladders while the first was being filled.

They waited ten minutes but the servant had not returned. Margaret wrapped the full bladder in her handkerchief and left it in the shop telling Mr Weaver she would return immediately with the other bladders and pay for all three gallons. Some time passed and the suspicious shopkeeper opened the bladder wrapped in her handkerchief and found that his brandy had become treacle and water.

Mr Weaver's young daughter went out asking after the woman and about an hour later, by a stroke of good fortune, found her leaving a house in one of the Water Lanes where she had been offering her brandy for sale. She was soon arrested. At the next Quarter Sessions it was stated that she had tricked another spirit dealer earlier in the week. She was sentenced to be transported for seven years.

After the trial the *York Herald* published a warning to shopkeepers. It might have been better advised to warn its readers of the dangers of the infamous Water Lanes which we shall visit shortly.[1]

Caution to Publicans
1849

A shabby-looking man called James Sadler entered the Queen's Head, Fossgate, called for a glass of brandy, drunk it and then said he had no money.[2]

The drunken dodger
1850

On Wednesday 28 November waterman John Taylor stood at the Guildhall charged with attempting to drown himself by throwing himself in the River Ouse at King's Staith while in a state of intoxication. He had been thrown out of the *Fortunate Tar* on King's Staith. Outside, the river was in flood, as it often is today, and was almost at the level of the footpath. As landlord Mr Demain turned to go back inside he heard a loud cry and saw that his unwanted customer was in the water.

In court he described the cry as drunken nonsense, calculated to disturb other people, and told the magistrates that Taylor had no intention of drowning himself. He said it was merely a dodge to obtain a glass of hot water and brandy, but instead he got a good dousing of cold water and mud. The magistrates agreed. They ordered Taylor to pay 5s and costs or to go to the House of Correction for seven days where, instead of brandy and water, he would receive the latter in its purity.[3]

A virtuoso performance at *The Clock*
1825

On Friday 12 August Mrs Dickinson was looking after business at *The Clock* in Walmgate in her husband's absence. A well-dressed man walked in and ordered a glass of second-rate gin, known at the time as 'blue ruin'. The inn was not busy and in his conversation with Mrs Dickinson the visitor told her he was one of the Oldbuck school, a reference no doubt to the character Jonathan Oldbuck in Sir Walter Scott's *The Antiquary* published some nine years before. He said he was a collector of old coins and asked if he could search in her till for antique pieces to enrich his collection cabinet. She left him to his task as he eagerly rummaged through every halfpenny and silver coin, carefully examining each one. While he was searching she noticed that the amount of money in the till seemed to be growing less, but she was so impressed with his demeanour that she allowed him to continue.

When he had finished he told her that he had found nothing of interest but, as he turned to leave two or three coins fell from out of his sleeve onto the floor. Mrs Dickinson finally plucked up the courage to challenge him and threatened to call the police. He protested indignantly. 'How can you possibly doubt the intentions of so philosophical a gentleman as myself?' Intimidated, she allowed him to leave.

On his return home, Mr Dickinson counted the money in his till. The sum of 7s 6d was missing and it seems the swindling virtuoso was never caught. A warning was issued to tradesmen.[4]

A carman's trick
1842

It happened one day last week that a gentleman and a lady, apparently strangers, emerged from the White Swan Inn in Pavement and addressing a cabman whose vehicle was standing opposite asked him if he could direct them the way to the White Horse in Coppergate.

This worthy, who is known among his brethren of the whip by the sobriquet of Jem Crow, with an eye to business respectfully touched his hat and smiling said 'Perhaps you would like to go in a cab sir?'

The gentleman asked the fare and on being told a shilling the party took their seats in Jem's convenience, who with a flourish of the whip forthwith mounted the box and off he went up Parliament Street, down Jubbergate, up Spurriergate and Nessgate, merrily wheeling past the corner into Coppergate, thus 'Turn about, round about, jumps Jem Crow', until he set down his fare at their desired hostel not more than forty yards from the place where he so kindly took them up.[5]

'Perhaps you would like to go in a cab sir?'

Fools and their money
1850

One Monday in September Thomas Atkinson, described as an old man from Cattal 'on whose brows appeared the frosts of age', presented himself before the magistrates at the Guildhall where he accused a young lady of robbery and her male accomplice of receiving the stolen goods. He claimed that Catherine Herbert had stolen his watch, a sovereign, two half-sovereigns and about £1 in silver coins and given them to John North, but he seemed reluctant to say more.

With great difficulty magistrate Meek managed to establish that on the Saturday night the old man had been at the *Square and Compass* where he had drunk two or thee pints of ale and went upstairs to eat his tea. He was followed by a woman whom he said he had known for a year or two as she used to come into the house when he was there.

Suspecting the nature of the young lady's profession Mr Meek asked him 'Did you send for this woman when you got into the public house?' 'Sent?' asked Mr Atkinson with a puzzled expression, causing some laughter among the spectators. 'No, she came there accidentally. I ordered some beefsteak and she had a bit with me.'

Magistrate Mr Mumby asked 'What made her go upstairs?' Atkinson said 'I don't know. I fell asleep and when I woke I'd lost my watch and money, and she'd gone.'

Mr Meek then took up the questioning: 'Did you know anything about going into the city and buying her a bonnet and a habit shirt?'

Atkinson – 'I never bought her a habit shirt.'

Mr Meek – 'Did you leave the public house and go into the city with this woman?'

Atkinson – 'I think perhaps I did.' (laughter)

Mr Meek – 'Did you go into the shop and buy her a bonnet?

Atkinson – 'Why, I don't know.'

Mr Meek – 'Now speak the truth!'

Atkinson – 'She got a bonnet of her own accord.'

Mr Meek – 'Who paid for it?'

'I never bought her a habit shirt'

Atkinson – 'I believe I did.' (renewed laughter)

Mr Meek – 'What drink had you after you left the public house?'

Atkinson – 'Not a sup. I went back to the *Square and Compass* and fell asleep while she was in the room.'

Mr Meek – 'You were very drunk were you not?'

Atkinson – 'I was sick.'

Mr Meek – 'When you awoke who was with you?'

Atkinson – 'A walk?' (laughter)

Mr Meek – 'No, awoke, wakened, that do you understand?' (renewed laughter) 'When you fell asleep this woman was in the room with you?'

Atkinson – 'Yes.'

Mr Meek – 'And no other person?'

Atkinson – 'The landlord had been in the room just before.'

Mr Meek eventually established that the old man had paid 5s for a gown, 4s for a shawl, and 2s for a bonnet.

Catherine Herbert said she had known Mr Atkinson for four years and he had also bought her the habit shirt and the pair of cuffs she was wearing. She said that her meeting with him that Saturday had been arranged the Sunday before, and that while they were in town he bought three of four drinks at two dram shops for her and another lady. When they were in the *Square and Compass* he was very tipsy and he gave her his watch and money to look after, as he had often done before.

Knowing there was no chance of a conviction, the magistrates felt they had no option but to dismiss the case.[6]

Won't you marry me?
1840

In the first half of the nineteenth century a public house called *The Marquis of Granby* stood half-way down Peter Lane, a narrow alley joining Market Street and Ousegate. It had previously been the *Golden Ball* but was re-named around 1770 on the death of the Marquis, a popular commander and benefactor of the British army. By 1855 it had become *The Griffin* and its reputation for attracting notorious characters grew to such an extent that it was closed by the magistrates in 1870.

Back in 1840 Miss Leach, a young servant girl, worked here. One day in September one of the regular customers, a moulder, asked her to marry him. Flattered and overjoyed, she hurried out to buy a marriage licence and the following morning the knot was tied at the altar of nearby All Saints' church. The wedding service went smoothly although afterwards the groom forgot to pay the wedding fee to the vicar. The reason for this became apparent the next day for while the groom was enjoying a drink in *The Marquis of Granby* in walked his first wife with their child. The poor servant girl was devastated and all the moulder could do was to beg her forgiveness saying it was only a drunken spree. The press reported that Miss Leach accepted his apology, but made no comment as to whether his wife was so forgiving.[7]

CHAPTER 3

At Home in the Inn

An envelope marked 'poison'
1861

At about 10.45 on an August evening, sixteen-year-old Ann Blain stood at the door of the *Bricklayer's Arms* in Walmgate with her boyfriend, Bob Birch. The two had been courting for the past two years. Ann's father, William, who was the inn's landlord, called her in to bed. Ann came in, lit a candle to see her way, turned off the gas lamp and locked the dram shop. She then went upstairs to her bed, in the same bedroom as her parents and their two younger children who slept at the other end of the room.

During the night, Mr and Mrs Blain were awakened by Ann calling out, 'You said I shall not have Bob'. Mr Blain answered, 'What have we to do with Bob?' and they drifted back to sleep. Soon afterwards they were awakened by Ann screaming 'Lord have mercy upon me! Lord have mercy upon my soul!' Mrs Blain got out of bed and went across the room to her daughter. 'William,' she called, 'She's in a fit. Get up.' He went over to her and lifted her up and asked, 'Have you taken anything?' 'Yes,' she answered, 'Poison.' 'Whatever has made you do this to bring such a disgrace upon your parents?' he demanded and she said to him 'Nowt through you father, nowt through you'. William dressed quickly and ran out to find a doctor. Dr Alfred Ball arrived to find Ann propped up in a chair by her mother and young Bob. He gave her a strong emetic but it did not produce vomiting and he could not get the stomach pump to work as her teeth were so firmly clenched.

By 2 o'clock in the morning Ann had died. Her parents later went down into the dram shop where William found an envelope labelled 'Wilde's instantaneous vermin and insect killer'. It was marked 'Poison'. His wife found a glass with a few drops in the bottom.

At the inquest in the inn the following Wednesday Dr Ball said he thought she had taken ten grams of strychnia and one and a half would have been enough to kill an adult.

Bob told the jury 'She left the house while I was there to fetch some rat poison from Frederick Leak's shop in Walmgate for her father, to kill the rats in the cellar. She'd been very low-minded since Sunday night. I cannot tell why.' Mr Leak was asked about restrictions on the sale of poison and said the only one for which sales were regulated was arsenic. Ann's father said, 'A bad woman reported that my daughter was in the family way. That was not the case, she was a modest girl. The report got all over York. She thought people looked at her as she walked in the street. Every day she used to talk about it.' He added 'No quarrel had taken place between her and Birch. She had never been forbidden to keep his company and I think about him as my own son.' Within a year or two William and his family left the *Bricklayer's Arms*.[1]

'I'm going to drown myself'
1844

Elizabeth Warrington had been working for four or five months as a nanny for landlord Richard English, who kept an inn in Davygate. The twelve-year-old had been back to live with her stepfather, John Neeson, in North Street for a few days to look after her sick mother, but she returned to the inn because she was better fed there than at home. Her life at the inn was not a happy one. On a Wednesday evening in June she was down at the riverside with her friend Ann Linfoot and was so afraid of being punished for being late home that she said she would rather drown herself. Ann persuaded her to go home but when she arrived the landlord's wife flogged her over her back until her nose bled.

A few days later, at about 7 o'clock in the evening, she was walking by the riverside again at the bottom of Marygate with her sister Jane and her friends Elizabeth McGreaves, who also lived in Davygate, and Sarah Robinson. They had the landlord's child with them. It got to 8.30 before Elizabeth Warrington realised how late it was. She picked up the child, gave it two kisses and placed it on the ground by the

They were unable to save her

hedge. She then sat down and started to take off her boots. Her friend Elizabeth asked, 'What are you going to do?'

'I'm going to drown myself,' she replied. Her friend said, 'No, come home,' but she answered 'No I daren't, I shall get flogged for being out so long.'

Meanwhile, Mrs English had sent her husband to find the children, and just as Elizabeth had taken off her boots she saw him walking towards her. She immediately leapt into the river. Mr English and his companion James Wyrill tried to get her out of the water but were unable to save her. At the inquest at the *Bay Horse* in Marygate a verdict was given that she had drowned herself in a state of temporary insanity.[2]

'Dear mother'
1885

More than forty years later we meet another young servant girl living in fear of her employer. Twenty-year-old Jane Lund had worked at the *Bay Horse* in Fulford for three or four months in the service of landlord Henry Ridsdale and his wife. At about 8.30 in the evening on 26 August she was washing the kitchen floor and she told the landlady 'I shall soon have done, I shan't be long now' and Mrs Ridsdale retired upstairs because of her rheumatism. When she came down about an hour later Jane was missing. Jane had asked for some time off earlier that day to go to the races, but the landlady had refused and some harsh words had been spoken between them. Mrs Ridsdale made some enquiries about Jane and hearing nothing she thought that she must have gone to her sister's house on the other side of town.

One afternoon, about a week later, William Press and Samuel Mills were sailing the barge *Duke of York* and discovered a body floating in the river. They recovered it and carried it in their vessel to Fulford landing, from where PC Clarke had it taken to the *Bay Horse*. It was identified there as Jane.

On her body were found some letters and some tradesmen's bills. One of the letters, in her own hand, read 'Dear mother, just a few lines as it will be the last I shall write. Think on and get my clothes. Good night and God bless you. There is a pair of new boots and a new frock. Think on and get them. It was the mistress that caused me to do it.'[3]

A miraculous recovery
1829

At Christmas 1828 a girl in the service of Mr Drummond of the *Sportsman's Arms* caught a very severe cold which ended in an almost total deprivation of speech and the poor girl could only give out a quiet whimper. Several eminent medical practitioners tried their skill but eventually the girl's case was considered hopeless.

Towards the end of July the following year the landlord's wife had been on a visit to Scarborough and brought back some sea water for the girl to drink. It was reported that within two or thee days she had completely recovered her powers of speech.[4]

Too fond of the bottle
1854

Sisters-in-law Hannah and Elizabeth Thompson were servants at William Mountain's *Cross Keys* in Goodramgate. After they had announced their intention to leave, William noticed that several items were disappearing and on a Wednesday afternoon in June he asked if he could search their personal boxes. They felt that they could not object and in the boxes he found some candles, soap, sugar, a brooch and a gold seal. He called PC Wright who found two bottles of brandy and two of gin hidden under their mattresses. The two women were charged by the magistrates the next day and were sent for trial.[5]

The embezzlers
1843

Thomas Winn of the *George Hotel* had fared no better with his servants some eleven years earlier. Henry Wear had been working in the hotel as a waiter for the past few months but had recently fallen out with one of the chambermaids. He decided to leave and per-suaded his fellow-waiter Thomas Powlett, who had worked there for three or four years, to do the same and on Monday evening 3 July off they went, apparently without giving notice.

Searching a drawer which had been used by Henry Wear, the landlord found two letters, one addressed to him and signed by both of the waiters, and one to Henry Wear's uncle. The letter to the land-lord politely announced that the two had taken with them a con-siderable sum of money.

The police caught up with the pair and searched their pockets. On Thomas Powlett they found only 1s 4d in silver and 2d in copper, but his accomplice was carrying £18 10s in gold and 18s 6d in silver and copper, almost a year's wages. In defence he said that not all of the money belonged to the landlord; £5 or £6 of it belonged to the head waiter and that when the two of them absconded they had only taken about £26 between them.[6]

A magnificent dog
1848

> To be sold, a magnificent Newfoundland dog 2 feet 7 inches high and an excellent house and guard dog. Apply to the head ostler, the George Inn, Coney Street.[7]

An excellent house and guard dog

A bad-tempered cook
1853

Margaret Birbeck was a cook at the *George Hotel*. On Saturday 1 October she was trying to work in the kitchen and became increasingly annoyed with the scullery maid Ann Scaife, who was whitewashing the kitchen and carelessly, if not deliberately, sprinkling whitewash over the meat. Margaret took hold of a meat cleaver and seized Ann by the throat but, as the maid struggled for her life, the cleaver fell and cut her arm. Ann called out to the hotel manager and when Margaret saw him arrive she struck Ann over the head with a rolling pin threatening to give her something to get a summons for. The two women were separated and a policeman was called.

The next Monday, Margaret appeared in court. The Lord Mayor was told that she was a woman of a very violent temper. He was reminded that on a previous occasion she had taken Sarah Scawin, landlady of the *Railway Hotel*, to court and, upon losing the case, had

The maid struggled for her life

assaulted one of the gentlemen in court. The Lord Mayor caused uproarious laughter when he remarked that it was obvious that cooks were bad-tempered women for he had experienced it himself. He and his brother magistrates were of the opinion that the case had been made out and they fined Margaret 5s.[8]

Sarah's story
1852

Like many nineteenth century inns, the *Malt Shovel* in Walmgate had its own brewery. Some landlords employed brewers, but most, like John Brown who had recently taken over at the *Malt Shovel*, brewed their own beer. On the evening of 18 November he went to bed early, intending to get up at 3 or 4 o'clock the next morning when his next batch of beer would be ready. Meanwhile Mrs Brown was downstairs serving customers.

John's sleep was disturbed at 9 o'clock that evening and he woke up and called for his wife. She came into the bedroom and asked him how much money he had. He told her £4 16s. 'Well, there's only a pound and a few shillings on the table now,' she said. Mrs Brown told him she suspected their servant, forty-nine-year-old Sarah Wilson, who seems not to have been over-endowed with brains. Mr Brown told her to make sure Sarah did not leave the house. He quickly dressed and went downstairs to confront his servant, and in the presence of one of his neighbours, a Mr Taylor, he accused her of having been in his room. 'No I wasn't,' she said, and when the landlord said he had seen her she replied 'How could you see me when you were asleep?'

A policeman was sent for, and when PC Sweeting arrived she was handed over to him and taken to the police station. She told Mrs Whitwell, the searcher 'I've nothing on me, I'm not even worth a halfpenny', but while she was being searched two sovereigns wrapped in paper fell from her breast and Mrs Whitwell found another in Sarah's stocking. Sarah admitted 'I took it out of his pocket when he was at supper'.

Mrs Brown told the police that Sarah had asked whether the landlord had gone to bed yet, but she did not answer. She later heard someone in her husband's room, and found the door open, although it had been closed when he went to bed. Sarah told her 'You can't have heard me moving about in the room, only when I fell'. Mrs Brown had found Sarah without a candle in her own room, and Sarah had made a frivolous excuse for being there.

In court, Sarah was charged with having stolen three sovereigns and 8s. In defence she said 'I didn't take the money out of Mr Brown's pocket. I picked it up from the kitchen floor'. She did acknowledge that the money found in her clothing belonged to him and was given a two-month prison sentence with hard labour.[9]

'In with him!'
1837

Many inns had their own stables, the equivalent of modern-day car-parks, and landlords employed ostlers to attend to the horses. Coney Street's *George Hotel* was one of the city's largest coaching inns with forty bedrooms, a double coach-house and stabling for thirty horses. In 1837 the chief ostler here was Thomas Noble. On Thursday 17 August the Guildhall was crowded for the trial of six men accused of attempting to murder him. The six were Richard Jackson, Henry Carr, Thomas Hudie, Charles Spence, William Armitage and John Fade.

At about 4 o'clock in the afternoon of the previous Monday Hudie, who was also employed at the *George*, had been abusing Noble to one of his men in the inn yard. Noble told Hudie that his conduct was so bad that if he had anything to do with it he would have him sacked. Hudie threatened the ostler and then left.

At 10 o'clock that night, hearing noises in the yard, the ostler took a lantern to light the high lamp there, and as he climbed the ladder he heard someone close the large outer door behind him. He asked 'Who's there?', and a voice replied 'You shall know soon'. Immediately about a dozen men surrounded the ladder and Carr said 'Come down old fellow, we're toed to have thee'. Jackson said that if he didn't come down he would throw him off the ladder. He got about half way down when Jackson turned the ladder over and threw him upon the stones.

Jackson then grabbed him by the throat and Carr, Spence and Hudie dragged him across the yard. In the yard there was a large water cistern, said to be five feet seven inches deep, which was full to within about an inch and a half. Armitage stood by, encouraging them and shouting 'In with him', while Spence took the old ostler's legs and Fade held him from behind. As they threw him in he tried to catch the sides to save himself, but they kept beating him down and he was overturned twice. Several times he cried out 'Murder!' and after about five minutes the landlord, Abraham Braithwaite, and his wife and some others came to his rescue. They cried 'Shame!' at the men, who left the ostler splashing around in the cistern and ran off.

The next morning Armitage came into the yard and asked Noble how he had liked his bath. He added that if he had been one of the men who had put him in, he would have taken care that he did not

They took the ostler's legs and threw him in

come out alive. The next day, the day before they appeared in court, Armitage and Hudie said they were prepared to put Noble in the cistern again at 10 o'clock that night and Noble had to get a police-man to protect him. In spite of this, Armitage told the ostler that same night that he would drown him until he was dead.[10]

The ostler's new clothes
1857

Sixteen-year-old Charles Fearnley had been working for a few weeks at the *Spotted Dog* in St Saviourgate as an ostler. As well as looking after the horses he had a number of other duties including cleaning the bedroom windows.

On Friday 16 July, landlord John Hunt had placed twenty sovereigns in a cash box which he locked and left in a drawer in his bedroom. Two or three days later he discovered that three sovereigns were missing, but at the time did not know who to suspect. The following week more money was taken and Mr Hunt noticed that the boy now had a watch and new clothes.

Charles claimed to have bought the watch, but after being arrested he confessed to the theft of three sovereigns. In his possession were found two or three duplicate keys, which fitted the cash box, as well as a number of cigars which he had stolen from Mr Hunt.

The boy admitted his guilt in court the following Monday and the magistrates sentenced him to three months' hard labour.[11]

He had been working at the Spotted Dog *for a few weeks*

Window cleaning at the *Old George Hotel*
1870

Some thirteen years later another sixteen-year-old, William Anson, was employed as boots at the *Old George Hotel* which stood across Pavement facing down towards All Saints church. A sailor's son, William had chosen a job on land and for the past ten or eleven weeks had worked at the hotel, a short walk from his home in St Andrewgate.

The job of boots was one of the most menial at a hotel, cleaning the boots of customers and doing whatever odd jobs no-one else wanted. One of these, for young William, was to clean the windows and for the upper floors there was a piece of equipment called a monkey.

On 14 January William opened the third floor window nearest Fossgate and placed the monkey into position, but as he climbed out onto it he and the equipment fell into the street below. William had landed head-first and bystanders who rushed to his aid found him lying unconscious and bleeding heavily. They carried him into the hotel and medical help was sent for. Surgeon Baird was in the neighbourhood and soon arrived at the *Old George*, but he confirmed that William's skull was broken and that he was dead.

They carried him into the hotel

The coroner's jury agreed that William had not secured the equipment properly but said that the equipment was old and that the holes were too big for it to be fixed into. Their opinion was that the monkey was unfit for use and should not be used for cleaning windows again.[12]

A man respectable in his sphere
1816

As the first anniversary of the Battle of Waterloo was being celebrated in York by the ringing of bells and public feasting, the death was reported of John Sowry, 'a man respectable in his sphere'. John had been the ostler and brewer at the *Bird in Hand* in Bootham and had somehow fallen into a copper tank of boiling liquid. He was severely scalded but survived for two days before he passed away leaving a wife and two young children. The press reported that they were destitute of friends and pleaded for charitable help for them.[13]

On a Tuesday in June 1829, John Smith, brewer at the *Punch Bowl* in Thursday Market, went into the brewhouse there to clean the boiler in preparation for the next morning's brew. He had seemed to be in his usual good health but landlady Mrs Clapham realised that she could not hear him working and became concerned. After calling him several times, she asked someone to go into the brewhouse. They climbed the ladder to the top of the boiler and saw him inside at the bottom. The press reported bluntly that on being brought out he was a corpse.[14]

Forty-three-year-old John Clough worked in Mr Morrison's brewery in Tanner Row, close to his home. While he was brewing on the evening of Thursday 17 August 1850 his foot slipped and he fell into a tub filled 2 feet deep with hot beer. Stephen Ward, who was working with him, pulled him out as quickly as he could but John was covered in hot beer and badly scalded. He was taken home and attended by surgeon Keyworth and Dr Belcombe. For two or three days he seemed to be on the road to recovery, but he developed a slow fever and within a week of the accident he had died. The inquest was held in Joseph Eyre's *Yorkshire Tavern*, which soon afterwards became the *Yorkshire Hussar* and eventually the *First Hussar*.[15]

Some twenty-three years later, on a Thursday afternoon in August, sixty-nine-year-old Matthew Varey was working in the brewhouse of the *Coach and Horses* in Nessgate when he climbed a ladder to turn off some taps. He lost his footing and fell backwards, cracking his skull on the stone floor. His son saw the accident and rushed for assistance, but Matthew died within half an hour.[16]

A ferment amongst brewers
1829

On a Wednesday morning in early September the brewer arrived at the *Punch Bowl* in St Sampson's Square to find that there had been a break-in at the brewhouse the previous night. The thieves had stolen the yeast he had prepared for his day's work. The press wryly commented 'Such a species of theft is calculated to cause a ferment amongst brewers'.[17]

Notice

Whereas a grey horse was left at the Cross Keys, Dringhouses, on the 15th December 1799, and whereas it has been requested that the said horse might be released, notice is hereby given that unless he is taken away and all expenses paid for keeping etc. on or before 21st instant, he will then be sold by auction by L Lund at the Pavement Cross in York. Dringhouses, May 17th 1800.

A fatal fall at the *Cross Keys*
1888

The *Cross Keys* in Dringhouses, on the mail coach road from York to the south, was a well-known venue for horse trading with stables standing behind the inn. In later years the stables were used for race-horses and were pulled down in 1965, two years after seven of the horses there were mysteriously poisoned. In 1888, fifty-three-year-old Thomas Ellis was landlord here and he was also a well-known horse dealer working as an agent for the London firm of Philips and East.

The Cross Keys, *named in honour of St Peter, York's patron saint*

On the night of Thursday 1 May he was standing at the top of the narrow stairs, which had a sharp bend in them, when he suffered a fit and fell to the bottom. Dr Petch and a surgeon were sent for and when the doctor arrived he found the landlord lying at the foot of the stairs, propped up with pillows and covered in blankets. His right leg was broken in two or three places.

The day after his fall Mr Ellis became delirious and permanent sickness set in, and within four days he had died. At the inquest Dr Petch said that the landlord's death had been a result from shock following the accident.[18]

Tragedy at the *Lord Nelson*
1865

Behind the *Lord Nelson* in Walmgate was a long yard and below it a garden leading down to the River Foss. At the bottom of the garden were two steps where fifty-one-year-old landlord Robert Calvert often stood to get water from the river to water his garden, and sometimes he fed the swans from there.

Shortly before 5 o'clock on Saturday afternoon of 26 August he was in the kitchen, stirring chopped pork with his bare hands, and then decided to go out into the garden. When his daughter, Annie, asked him where he was going he told her he was going to see the young pigs he kept locked up in a loose box. She tried to persuade him not to go but he said he had not checked on them since lunchtime and asked her to fetch the key. She gave him the key and as he walked towards the loose box her mother called her inside.

After about ten minutes Annie went out into the garden to look for her father and was horrified to find him lying in the river with his hands and feet out of the water. She ran back to the house screaming and the ostler, Henry Fusedale, hurried down to the river where he found Robert a few feet out into the river, floating on his back with his nose and lips just above the surface. As the ostler pulled him out Robert's eyes moved and Henry thought he felt a quiver at the back of the landlord's neck. There still seemed some hope of saving him and surgeon Allen was sent for. The surgeon tried artificial respiration but there was no sign of any breathing, nor was there any heartbeat, and the surgeon pronounced him dead. Policeman Kinson searched Robert's pockets, finding a silver watch, a pair of spectacles, 8s and 1½d in silver and copper and a handkerchief.

Initially the press had reported suicide but at the inquest the jury were told that Robert had appeared cheerful that afternoon and it was likely that he had gone down to the river to wash his hands and fallen in. A verdict of accidental death was given.[19]

CHAPTER 4

Dangerous Times

Death in a cesspool
1850

Young Henry Parker worked at Mr Graves' grocer's shop in High Ousegate. Each morning he would walk the short distance from his home in Hungate to start work at 7 o'clock. Close to where he lived, in a dark corner below a house in Garden Place, there was a public privy, and on Thursday morning, 5 September, Henry called in on his way to work. He pushed the door open and was horrified to see the body of a man partly immersed in the large cesspool in the floor. He ran to tell William Reed, a tailor who lived in Garden Place and someone was sent to find a policeman.

Policeman Catton was on duty in Pavement and came quickly to the scene. He asked for a light and went into the privy to investigate. It seemed that the man had fallen backwards into the cesspool. He was lying with his head against the opposite wall, with his legs stretched out on the floor and the foul liquid covering his left arm, shoulders, neck and face up to his mouth. One of his braces was unbuttoned and his hat was lying beside him. He was a tall stout man, apparently dead and stiffened, and he was stuck fast in the hole. With great difficulty the policeman pulled him out and he was taken into the *Wheatsheaf Inn* and placed in warm water but he could not be revived. Meanwhile policeman Catton had the dubious pleasure of searching the man's sodden pockets and found a half crown, five pence in copper, eight pledge tickets and some other articles.

The policeman pulled him out

That afternoon the inquest was held at the *Wheatsheaf*. The body
was identified as Charles Lacy, a joiner. His brother said he was aged
about thirty or thirty-two and had lately been given to intemperate
habits. The previous afternoon Charles had been drunk at the *Sportsman's Arms* in Hungate and at 5 o'clock had fallen asleep there. The
landlord, Thomas Wade, had asked Edward Turpin, his groom, to
wake him and see him out. Charles had returned to the inn shortly
after 10.30 but found the door closed so he walked along Hungate to
the privy. His landlady, Mrs Kilner, said Charles had been in the
habit of sleeping in a privy in Stonebow, but recently the door had
been locked at night.

Surgeon Allen told the jury that the body was badly discoloured
from sulphurated hydrogen which was poisonous enough to kill anyone who had stayed in the privy all night. He said that anyone entering
the privy might be seized with giddiness and fall into the hole in the
floor, from which they would be unable to get out. On hearing this,
some of the jury said that there were similar privies in the area and
were in favour of a verdict of gross neglect against the owners. They
trusted that the proper steps would now be taken.[1]

A dangerous privy at the *John Bull*
1864

At 6 o'clock on a Saturday afternoon in May, fifty-seven-year-old
labourer George Dunning walked unsteadily into the *John Bull* and
asked landlady Mrs Hutchinson to lend him a shilling. Seeing how
drunk he was, she refused and told him to go home to his family.

Before he left he went down the yard behind the inn to use the
privy at the edge of the river bank. A neighbour, Mrs Bradley, heard
shouting from the direction of the river and rushed into the *John Bull*
to raise the alarm. Three customers ran down to help and managed to
pull his body from the water and take it back inside.

At the inquest there the next Monday evening it was mentioned
that another man had met his death in similar circumstance three
years before. It was said how dangerous the yard was, as the descent
was very steep and the gaslight was on the opposite bank. It was
recommended that the river should be fenced. George left several
small children who were now orphans.[2]

The steps at the *Crown & Anchor*
1873

On Friday 12 December seventy-year-old widow Caroline Brown was
leaving the *Crown & Anchor*. Being close to the river, the pub was
often threatened by flooding and was accessed by two flights of steep

The riverside Crown & Anchor

unprotected stone steps. In the dark cold night Mrs Brown lost her footing and fell. She was carried back to her lodgings badly shaken and the next day Dr Hood found that she had broken her thigh. At the inquest on her death it was recommended that a rail or banister should be fitted. Twelve years later the pub was demolished.[3]

The old stables at the *White Horse*
1859

In the yard of the *White Horse* in Coppergate there was an old six-stalled stable owned by Mr Craven who also owned the neighbouring confectionery factory. George Pearson, aged about thirty-seven, worked as ostler at the inn and between 10 and 11 o'clock on a Saturday morning at the beginning of October he was un-harnessing a horse from a gig, close to the old building. Suddenly the roof of the stable fell, taking with it several feet of bricks from the upper part of the wall. George was almost buried by bricks and tiles and one of Mr Craven's factory workers, Robert Clark, ran to his aid. Some people helped him to extricate George, who was badly injured and bleeding from the head. He was rushed to York County Hospital where his leg was amputated and he died the following evening.

At the inquest in the *Turk's Head* in College Street the following Wednesday evening, Mr Craven and George Ward, the landlord of the *White Horse*, both stated that they had not considered the stable to be in a state of disrepair. The coroner, J P Wood, disagreed and said the other buildings in the *White Horse* ought to be thoroughly examined by proper workmen.

The jury gave a verdict of accidental death on George, who was said to have been the only support of an aged mother.[4]

Excavations in the cellar
1839

In 1838 William McLaren opened the *Burns Coffee House* in Market Street and began rebuilding the premises to turn it into a hotel. For several weeks workmen had been excavating the cellar to prepare for a new house to be built next door. At the back of the cellar there was a wall, a foot thick, which Mr McLaren had considered to be dangerous, but nothing had been done to make it safe because of a dispute over to whom the wall belonged. Between 9 and 10 o'clock on a Saturday evening in February, the wall was showing signs of collapsing and a messenger was sent to the bricklayer to have it secured. While this was happening a servant girl was in the cellar cleaning shoes and the wall collapsed beside her. The press reported that she had narrowly escaped being killed and that the dispute over ownership had been resolved by an agreement to build a party wall.

William continued to run the *Burns* until his death in 1855 when his widow Sarah took over, remaining in business until she died at the age of seventy in 1879. During her time as landlady the original premises were acquired by a bank and she moved next door to the house which became the *Hansom Cab*.[5]

The wall in *Star Inn* passage
1846

The pub now called *Ye Olde Starre Inn* claims to have the city's oldest continuous licence and also its oldest inn sign. It is a 'gallows' sign, placed across the street in 1733 when a house was built in front of the inn obscuring it from view. Consequently, *The Star* is reached from Stonegate through a narrow walled passage and a small yard now used as one of its three beer gardens.

On Thursday, New Year's Eve, two boys named John Dearlove and Henry Rodwell were working in *Star Inn* passage. They had been employed by Mr Robinson of Stonegate, a hosier, and were using a wheelbarrow to clear snow from the passageway into the inn yard. A wall 9 feet high and about 12 yards long separated the passage from the adjacent property and as the boys were wheeling the barrow the wall collapsed burying both of them in snow and rubble. Henry escaped with a cut forehead and bruising to his foot but John was knocked unconscious suffering three or four broken ribs and other injuries. He was carried in a chair to hospital and detained there until he recovered.[6]

A fall from the walls
1857

Nine-year-old Roland Johnson lived in Barker Lane, a narrow street some yards from Micklegate bar. One day in August he was playing with a friend behind the *Jolly Bacchus* when he bet the other boy a penny that he could drop from the bar walls, a feat he had performed twice before. He had been seized with a fit on both of these occasions, but undaunted he was determined to earn his pocket money. He hung on tightly to the edge of the wall, planning his fall, but lost his grip and fell into the moat below where he lay quite still. Hs friend ran away but a boy named Charles Wells found him and ran to a railway-man for help. The man told Charles he did not like to see anyone dead, but Charles eventually found help and Ronald was carried into the *Jolly Bacchus* where a surgeon pronounced that his neck was broken and that he was dead. The inquest was held in the *Jolly Bacchus* where a verdict of accidental death was given. A newspaper report called for this section of wall to be fenced to prevent further incidents.[7]

Thirty-five years earlier an old widow had suffered a fatal fall from the same stretch of walls. Eighty-year-old Mrs Douglas was taking a summer Sunday evening walk with her friend when she slipped and fell onto the mound below. The press reported 'She spoke no more and within five minutes she was a corpse'. It added 'The ruinous state of our bar walls is a matter of most serious complaint by the inhabitants who are deprived from enjoying, with any tolerable degree of safety, a walk affording the most pleasing prospect and most salubrious air'.[8]

An explosion at *The Falcon*
1847

Gas-lighting was introduced on the streets of London in 1807 and by 1824 the York Gas Light Company had begun to supply lighting in the York streets.

In July 1847 York workmen had been replacing the narrow gas pipes with wider ones along Micklegate. It seems that their workmanship was not of the best standards and within a week of the job being

Ignorant of the properties of gas

completed there was a smell of escaping gas. Late one evening, a customer at *The Falcon* discovered the smell coming from a grate in the passage of the inn connecting with the drains. Ignorant of the properties of gas, he brought a lighted candle and held it over the grate to try to discover the source. The gas immediately ignited. He was injured by the explosion, which lifted the flagstones in the passage and spread into the street, blowing the top off a grate in Barker Lane. Alarmed neighbours poured out into the street but the gas was soon burnt out and the press reported that the astonished multitude peaceably retired to dream of dangers past and of horrid scenes that might have been.[9]

A lighted candle at the *Black Horse*
1842

At about midnight on a Thursday in November, Mary Ann Walton returned to her lodgings at the *Black Horse* in Fossgate. She had been to a ball in the neighbourhood – the press described her as 'a woman of the town' and implied that the nature of the ball befitted her character. The worse for drink, she managed to light her foul-smelling tallow candle and as she negotiated the dark stairway to her room she somehow managed to set her clothes on fire. Landlord

William Smith and his wife rushed to her assistance, fearing that the whole of the inn would be destroyed by the fire, and succeeded in extinguishing the flames but burned their hands very badly. Mary Ann was in a dreadful state with her skin literally burned off her arms, legs and shoulders and surgeon Abbey said he held out little hope for her recovery. The press made their own enquiries about her health the following evening, and were pleased to report that she was a little better.[10]

The Leeds Volunteers
1804

In the early part of the nineteenth century there was no official fire brigade in the city, but help was often at hand, sometimes from unexpected quarters. One Saturday evening in April a fire broke out in the stables adjoining the *Black Bull Inn* in Thursday Market. Neighbours came to assist, along with members of the Leeds Volunteers who were half-way through their month's stay in the city. Many of them would have been billeted in local inns. The soldiers were praised for their good orderly conduct and the way they helped to extinguish the blaze before the fire was able to spread.[11]

Horses from the *Black Swan*
1820

In October 1820 James Barber of the *Black Swan* in Coney Street sent horses for the fire engine to attend to a dreadful fire at Simpson's corn mill across the bridge in North Street. It was reported that two people had already died, Thomas Walker, aged fifteen, and the seven-year-old daughter of a butcher, and two more were unlikely to survive. The press gave a long list of casualties.[12]

Less than four years later the Yorkshire Insurance Company was founded by a group of businessmen in the *York Tavern*, close to the *Black Swan*. Metal fire marks depicting the York Minster emblem of the company were displayed on the walls of buildings to show that the company insured them. The fire brigades employed by the insurance companies were there to extinguish fires in the property they insured, protecting the shareholders' investments.

The Yorkshire Fire and Life Insurance Office
York, May 24th 1824

The establishment of such an office in the city of York, as the capital and central resort of this great agricultural and commercial county, being considered desirable and likely to conduce to the advantage of the

---

insurers, the insured and the public, it is requested that friends to such an institution will meet at the York Tavern on Monday 14th June 1824 at twelve noon to consider the most expedient means of carrying it into effect.

Those who approve of the measure are also required to signify their names to the bank of Messrs Raper, Swann & Co., York.

On Tuesday 14 July 1831 there was a fire in a stable belonging to the *Black Swan* in Coney Street, now displaying the York Minster emblem. It was reported that the timely arrival of engines and the prompt assistance of a number of people who were on the spot prevented the fire from spreading. The £80 worth of damage was insured by the Yorkshire Fire Office.[13]

The Black Swan, *its site is now marked by a plaque*

Two careless servants
1836

At about 1.30 on a January morning, two servant girls were sleeping at *The Greyhound* in Spurriergate and awoke to find their room enveloped in smoke and the clothes around them in flames. A prompt supply of water soon extinguished the fire but the press commented that 'The circumstances had no doubt arisen from the carelessness of these servants and we trust that it will operate as a caution to those who are entrusted with lights when going to bed'.

The remarks might have been fuelled by an incident earlier that month. At about 5 o'clock one Thursday evening a servant girl left the tap room of the *Robin Hood* in Castlegate and went upstairs with a lighted candle. When she reached the landing the flame was blown out and she went into the front bedroom to re-light the candle. Above the fire, a chemise and a petticoat were hanging up to dry. As she lighted a stick from the fire, sparks set the clothes alight. She immediately gave the alarm, but when several firemen arrived with their engine the fire had already been put out.[14]

Accidentally burnt
1851

In the *Coach & Horses* in Swinegate Mrs Kirk carried her three-month-old daughter Mary upstairs and gently placed her in the bed. It was Thursday 9 January and the sparkling fire in the bedroom had been newly lit to keep out the winter cold. A few minutes later Mrs Kirk heard crying and went back upstairs to find the bedclothes ablaze. She snatched up her daughter, and found that her own dress had also caught fire. She managed to put out the flames but was too late to save her child. The inquest was held at the inn some five weeks later, and a verdict was given of 'accidentally burnt'.[15]

Escape across the rooftops
1853

At 6.45 on a February morning flames were seen blazing out of one of the windows on the third storey of premises in Davygate, attached to *Harker's Hotel*.

A commercial traveller who had been sleeping on the floor above hastily dressed himself and ran down the stairs but the flames drove him back. He opened a window and cried for help, but it seemed that he could not be rescued. There was a lower adjoining roof covered with snow. He leapt onto it but slipped, lost his balance, and fell into the yard below. His fall was cushioned by the thick snow lying in the yard and he escaped without breaking any bones.

He leapt onto the roof, but slipped

Three fire engines of the Yorkshire Insurance Company arrived. The fire fighters quickly put out the fire but the furniture in five or six of the bedrooms was partially damaged and in two or three more was totally consumed by the flames and the floor was burnt through. It was reported that the cause of the fire was unknown and the damage was estimated at £250.[16]

Owned by Christopher Harker, a former butler, the hotel had been built in 1770 as the *York Tavern* with stabling for 150 horses. It stood for 160 years on the site since occupied by *Betty's* café and tea rooms.

A dead parrot
1863

At about midnight on Wednesday, 27 August, at the *Cross Keys* in Goodramgate William Mountain and his family had just retired to bed when they were alarmed by a strong smell of burning. Mr Mountain went back downstairs and into the back kitchen, where he found that some clothes left on two clothes horses in front of the fireplace were in flames. Some of the woodwork was already charred and the house would soon have been ablaze if he had not discovered the blaze in

The only casualty was a parrot

time. The only casualty was a parrot, which had been left in a cage in the kitchen and had been suffocated by the dense smoke.[17]

Seven horses burned to death
1866

The consequences of a fire three years later at the *Lion & Lamb* were more serious. Shortly after 5 o'clock on Monday afternoon 30 October a group of eight horses were being led to London from a great horse fair in Newcastle and their attendant Sam stopped at the inn in Blossom Street to stable them in the yard to the rear. The side and back of the stables were brick, and the roof tiled, but the front into the yard was wood. It was already dark and Sam worked by candlelight. He had just retired to rest in the early hours of the morning when a cry of fire was raised. Sam ran down to the stables and succeeded in getting into one of the stalls and setting two horses loose but one fell down dead in the yard. The others died in their stalls. The cause of the fire was unknown but it was thought one of Sam's candles might have fallen into the loose straw.[18]

After the Minster fire
1840

On 28 May the York Courant carried a report of 'the late dreadful fire in York Minster' with a large and detailed engraving of the building in flames. The previous column gave a story of two policemen Cruiss and Gladin, who were coming off duty at 7 o'clock in the morning after attending the fire and had visited the nearby *Star Inn* for some refreshments. When they arrived, the landlady asked them to turn out one of her customers, Thomas Dale who, she said, was disorderly. Dale told the policemen they had arrested him once and they would not do it again. He hit Cruiss, then knocked Gladin down and seized him by his throat and began to hit him.

In court Dale produced a witness to say the two policemen were drunk as they were walking down Stonegate towards *The Star*, and he also claimed that they had beaten him violently in *The Star* and on the way to the police station. Although the police sergeant said four policemen had left the Minster at 6.30 and all were sober at the time, the magistrates dismissed the case in view of the evidence against them.[19]

CHAPTER 5

The Visitors

Chimney sweeps at the *Coach & Horses*
1854

The *Coach & Horses* stood on the corner of Nessgate and Ousegate. A four-storeyed building, it had been a notable coffee house in the eighteenth century and later became a nine-bedroomed commercial hotel. Despite its name, it was never a coaching inn, but coaches sped past the busy corner throughout the day. The old building was eventually demolished in 1904 so that the street could be widened for the passage of trams, and a new inn of the same name rebuilt.

Fifty years earlier, on Tuesday morning, 5 September, two boys, named Watson and Murray, had been sent by Henry Varley to sweep

Despite its name, it was never a coaching inn

the chimney there. They had brought with them a machine which he told them to use, but when they arrived they found it was too short. Rather than return for more sticks, the younger boy decided to climb the chimney to sweep it.

When it was discovered that they had taken this risk Henry Varley was summoned to appear in court two days later, accused of allowing two persons aged under twenty-one to ascend a chimney to clean it. Landlord Joseph Giddy also had to appear, but he said the sweep was ordered by his wife and he had not known the chimney had been swept until he received his summons.[1]

A pie boy at the *Star & Garter*
1863

On the same block as the *Coach & Horses* stood a small single-fronted pub bearing the grand name of the *Star & Garter*. Ten-year-old Henry Turner was the son of a pie dealer and spent his evenings selling hot pies at public houses. Although he had been told repeatedly by landlord Edward Williamson not to hawk his pies at the *Star & Garter* he persisted in visiting the house. On Thursday 6 August he was back and the landlord asked him if he had any apple dumplings then told him to go away. Before the boy got out of the door the landlord called him back, asked him again if he had any apple dumplings, and threw water over him, presumably much to the delight of his customers.

In court the following Monday the magistrates ordered the landlord to pay costs and cautioned the boy's father not to allow him to go to houses where he had been requested to stay away.[2]

'Do you have any apple dumplings?'

A boy with a hand cart
1843

James Medford was aged about fourteen and was the son of a fish-dealer. On mornings when the fish market was held he would call at the *King's Arms* near Foss Bridge to collect fish which were stored there for his father. On Sunday 12 February Robert Granger, the ostler, was surprised to see him arrive with his handcart at 10 o'clock in the evening. James told him that his father had been drinking all day and made him come to collect the fish early. The fish were kept in a hamper in one of the stables, and Robert helped James carry the hamper out and load it onto the cart. As the ostler turned round to close the door James remarked that the hamper should be further forward and he stood on one of the shafts to move it. Robert heard him cry out 'Oh Dear!', or words to that effect, as he fell forward onto the front of the spindled cart. He asked James if he had hurt himself but the boy lay still and did not speak. He lifted him and laid him on the cart seeing to his horror that the front of the cart was broken and that the boy was bleeding profusely. He ran into the inn's bar, shouting that the boy had been killed. Landlord George Taylor came out into the yard with Robert and sent him for Dr Abbey.

The ostler was surprised to see him arrive

By the time Robert had returned with the doctor the boy had been taken inside. They saw that the rail of the cart had broken along with some of the spindles, one of which had penetrated deep into the boy's thigh. He was crying out in pain but could not speak. His father and mother arrived shortly after, but there was nothing the doctor could do, and at about midnight James died. The inquest was held in the inn the following day and a verdict of accidental death was given.[3]

The foreigner and the farmer
1858

At breakfast one morning at the quiet and comfortable old inn, the White Swan in York, a foreigner made a quick despatch with the eggs. Thrusting his spoon into the middle he drew out the yolk, devoured it and passed on to the next.

When he got to his seventh egg an old farmer, who had already been prejudiced against monsieur by his moustache, could brook the extravagance no longer and speaking up said 'Why sir, you have all the white! How is Mrs Lockwood to afford to provide breakfast at that rate?' 'Vy' replied the outside barbarian, 'you vouldn't have me eat de vite! De yolk is de shicken, de vite de fedders. Am I to make von bolster of my belly?' The farmer was dumbfounded.[4]

'Am I to make von bolster of my belly?'

A foreigner's gold watch
1851

It was reported that in June 1851 Mary and Thomas Smith appeared at the Guildhall charged with the theft of a foreigner's watch. The foreign gentleman was not named, possibly because his name was of no interest to the press readership, or more likely because the reporter was unable to spell it.

On the previous evening, a Monday, our visitor had been to a friend's house for tea and at about 10 o'clock on his way home some of his countrymen persuaded him to join them for a drink in the *Three Cups* at Foss Bridge. While he was dinking his gin and water he met the Smiths and Thomas asked him what time it was. He brought out his silver watch, and then his gold one, saying it kept much better time. After about twenty minutes he saw that his friends had left him and nervously finished his drink before leaving.

Outside it was raining heavily, but he was well prepared for the British summer and was carrying an umbrella which he offered to share with a lady sheltering at the door. When she left him he realised that his gold watch was missing. The Lord Mayor said that the evidence implied that the lady sharing his umbrella had taken it, but the foreign gentleman thought they were both involved. 'You missed your watch, but who got it?' the Lord Mayor asked him. 'I wish I knew, my lord' the man replied, to the laughter of the courtroom. He said that all he wanted was his watch back and asked the mayor to remand the prisoners until it could be found, but the mayor said there was nothing to justify holding them. He added that the police would do what they could and discharged the two accused.[5]

He offered to share his umbrella

CHAPTER 6

The Entertainers

Herr Dobler's dark séance
1872

On the afternoon of Wednesday 28 August some gentlemen took their seats in a darkened room in the *York Tavern*. All of the furniture had been removed, apart from a small table and the dozen chairs around it. For his paranormal performance, Herr Dobler had shut out all daylight.

The gas lights were extinguished for the rope trick, made famous by the Davenport brothers. After two minutes the lights were re-lit and Herr Dobler was found to be seated in his chair with his hands tied securely behind him and the rope leading down to his feet which were

It floated round the room with its bells tinkling

tied firmly to the chair legs. The guests carefully examined the rope around his wrists, then sealed the knots with wax.

They then returned to their seats to witness the 'floating instrument manifestation'. On the table lay a tambourine, which had been touched with phosphorous to be seen in the dark. The room was darkened again and the astonished audience watched the instrument rise from the table and float up over their heads and around the room, with its bells tinkling. In three or four minutes the gas lamps were lit and the tambourine was found to be lying near the door.

Herr Dobler, still tied in the chair, then asked one of the gentlemen for his coat. He took it across to the professor. Once more the lights were put out and when the room was illuminated Herr Dobler was wearing the coat, still tied in his chair with the sealing wax unbroken. The sequence was reversed and the audience watched the coat float through the air in the darkness.

The séance lasted about half an hour with the mystified audience believing that they had seen the performance of impossible feats of wizardry.[1]

The invisible lady
1802

The last day of exhibition in York at the Judges' Lodgings in Coney Street of the Invisible Lady. The proprietor and conductor of this novel experiment in optics and acoustics is proud to acknowledge the very flattering encouragement he has received in this city, particularly from a number of intelligent and scientific visitors who have recently honoured it with their attention.

To their testimony and opinion he refers the doubts of those who are unwilling to credit the voice of general report of those who still endeavour to account for the conversations of the invisible lady by the agency of ventriloquism. Those ladies and gentlemen who have not yet witnessed this singular exhibition are entreated not to lose the opportunity as it will most assuredly close this day.

The exhibition is open from 11 till 4 o'clock in the day and from 6 to 9 in the evening. Admission one shilling per person.[2]

The Judges' Lodgings moved to Lendal in 1806 and the old Coney Street premises became the *White Horse* coffee house. The proprietor, Mr T Crow, advertised his business to members of the legal profession and others attending the assize courts.

Transparent skin and hair as white as snow
1812

THE PUNCH BOWL, Stonegate

The nobility, gentry and public in general are most respectfully informed that those three beautiful Albinis are just arrived and to be seen at Mr Joy's Punch Bowl in Stonegate.

They are particularly worthy to the attention of all who delight in viewing such parts of the Creation as display the marvellous productions of Nature, their beauty cannot be credited but on sight.

They have been viewed with admiration, and particularly by the Faculty who have pronounced this to be truly the only living phenomena ever exhibited to the public.

To the ladies in particular the exhibition is recommended as nothing can display more innocence and beauty. Their skin is superior to waxwork, almost transparent, their hair nearly as white as snow, their eyes have a surprising sparkling lustre, quite different, far superior and more brilliant than any eyes ever beheld, with which the phenomena must show to the spectator the surprising and extraordinary work of nature.

And the like was never seen before. Miss Crawley is eleven years old, one boy nine and the other seven. The mother of the Albinis attends them.

Admittance to Ladies and Gentlemen one shilling each, servants and children sixpence.[3]

The previous week's edition of the *York Chronicle* advertised the visit to the city of Madame Tussaud's Grand European Carnival of Figures, consisting of sixty-nine public characters modelled from life. It was at the Dancing Room, previously Mr Goadby's dancing academy, in Goodramgate, open from 11 o'clock in the morning until 10 o'clock at night. Adults were charged 1*s*, children under ten, 6*d*.

The extraordinary work of Nature

A Polish dwarf
1803

Only 3 feet 3 inches high

> Count Boruwlaski, the Polish gentleman only 3 feet 3 inches high and aged 65 years has the honour to announce his arrival in York where he intends to receive company at Mr Birkett's cheesemonger in Jubbergate from 11 till 4 o'clock and from 5 until 7 in the evening. Admission 1/-.
>
> The count's memoirs to be had of him in French, written by himself, price 5 shillings. An English translation at the same price.[4]

Count Joseph Boruwlaski had toured the European courts meeting King George III, Maria Theresa, Voltaire and other celebrities and by 1803 he had moved to Durham where he gave concerts, dancing and playing the violin and guitar. He died at the age of ninety-seven and is buried in Durham Cathedral.

A living skeleton
1864

In April an inquest was held in John Brown's *Castle Inn* in Castlegate on the death of Robert Corbett who died in a house in the same street. Robert, aged thirteen or fourteen, was described as a 'living skeleton', 'the greatest sensation of the present day', 'a living miracle' and 'the wonder of the world'.

Two years before, his father had left Ireland for America, leaving his wife and two sons to fend for themselves. Since then Robert had been travelling the country on a salary of £3 a week with his agent Wilson and comedian John Shaw who earned 18s a week as doorman. He was being exhibited in an upstairs room at the back of the house to 'admiring thousands'. On the opening a curtain, Robert was to be seen seated on a sofa which was raised up against the wall like a throne. He was dressed in theatrical style with red leggings and a black velvet tunic ornamented with gilt.

At the inquest it was said that he was in a very emaciated state. His mother had been told that she should not be exhibiting him in such a state of health and she was reprimanded by the jury.[5]

Late night actors
1854

At 2 o'clock in the morning of Sunday 23 April 1854, police entered the *Queen's Head* in Bootham, not far from the Theatre Royal, and found several glasses and a pitcher of ale on the table. Landlord Lewis Hunter said that the whole of the party were theatricals, that four of them were lodgers, and the two other men their friends who had supper with them on their return from the theatre. The magistrates did not consider the case a very bad one and imposed a mitigated penalty of half a crown.

In a similar incident, late at night on Friday 23 May 1889, PC Alp went into the *Half Moon* in Blake Street and found several people drinking there after hours. The landlord Frederick Whitwell said that most of them were in the theatrical profession and engaged in the recent pantomime in York. They were there to raise a testimonial to Mr Williams who had played a leading role. He said that all of the drinks had been poured before 11 o'clock but the magistrates fined him 10s and each of the actors half a crown.

A month earlier the wife of landlord John Mason of the *Cattle Market* had to answer a similar charge. In the early hours of a Thursday morning a number of men connected with Savage's Circus were in the house taking refreshments before leaving the city. Mrs Mason said she did not think she needed a licence for this and the magistrates, probably taking the view that the men could be regarded as travellers, ordered her to pay only costs.[6]

A ghost in the house
1851

For more than a hundred years a house called the *Black Boy* had stood next to St John's church in North Street, but for a short time when Zachariah Whitehead was landlord it was named the *Hudson's Arms* after the man who brought York to prominence as a railway city.

The change of name did not change its reputation and towards the end of February 1851 the police received a tip-off that Mr Whitehead was conducting a disorderly house outside the terms of his licence. It was decided that in this case the presence of two officers would be too conspicuous so it was decided to send a policeman's wife and a boy. The lady worked at the police station carrying out body searches on female prisoners. They went to the house which was laid out as a small theatre and found that the admission charge was 1½d to the pit and 1d to the gallery. They paid the fee and went in to witness what appeared to be a spurious representation of Shakespeare's *Hamlet*. After about twenty minutes a policeman walked onto the stage to arrest the ghost, who tried to escape through a trapdoor but was arrested along with four other members of the York Theatricals.

The following Monday, a large crowd filled the Guildhall to witness their trial. The landlord was charged with allowing his house to be open as a public resort for the performance of stage plays without a licence. The magistrates said the Act for Licensing had been passed to prevent these indecent and improper representations which led to nothing but vice. It was not the first offence by the theatrical group and all five of the accused were bound over and threatened with a heavy penalty should they re-offend.[7]

Shakespearean celebrations
1863

On a Thursday evening, St George's Day, the anniversary of Shakespeare's birth and death, landlord Benjamin Barrett of the *Malt Shovel* in Fossgate delivered a lecture at his inn on the life of the bard. A large number of gentlemen had been invited and they listened to the landlord's presentation which was interspersed with some extracts from the most popular plays. It was reported that a very pleasant evening was spent and no doubt the audience were rewarded for their patience with ample food and drink.[8]

Leading young men into drunkenness
1869

While the rich of the city enjoyed their music and dancing at such venues as the Assembly Rooms, Victorian views on such frivolity among the poorer populace were less tolerant.

At the brewster sessions in 1869 Ralph Dean, landlord of *The Tiger* in Market Street, was taken to task. Neighbours had complained of singing and playing in the pub and claimed that this had a tendency to lead young men into drunkenness. In defence, Mr Dean told the licensing justices that the music always finished by 11 o'clock and that he discouraged young boys and refused to serve women. His licence was renewed on condition that there was no more music. This seems to have kept him on the right side of the law and five years later when police found two men stripped to the waist fighting in *The Tiger* the landlord was fined the minimum penalty and his licence remained clear.

Although York's pubs had only about a dozen music licences between them, many more landlords took the risk of providing singing and dancing, attracting perhaps fifty or more extra customers. By 1888 the new landlord, John Gretton, thought it was worth trying for a music licence for *The Tiger*, not in the pub, but in a separate back room in a different building partly occupied by a joiner's shop. His request was for public dancing, music and other entertainment, but eventually he asked for a singing licence only. He said he thought he would sell more drink if singing was allowed, and he would not allow females or soldiers. There was some doubt as to whether this part of the premises was covered by the drinking licence, and when an eagle-eyed neighbour reported that he had seen women and soldiers going down the passage into the room the application was refused.[9]

Leading young girls into bad company
1869

Also at the 1869 brewster sessions was a complaint that landlord Gill of *The Woodman* in Elmwood Street had permitted dancing and that this tended to lead young girls into bad company and ultimately to ruin. The Lord Mayor said he knew of an instance where ruin had been the result of frequenting *The Woodman* and Colonel Fitzwygram of the 15th Hussars said that but for *The Woodman* and another house in the neighbourhood he would require no walls to his barracks. The mayor then read three foolscap pages of reports which had been written about the house.

In defence, Mr Gill told him the girls who met in his house were not common to the street but milliners and dressmakers, but the mayor replied that this fact made the place even more dangerous. He said that only a few days ago a local tradesman had sacked his young lady assistant because she associated with characters in *The Woodman*.

The licence was withdrawn and although John Smith, the Tadcaster brewer, applied for the licence in his own name the following year it was not renewed.

Riotous dancing
1874

Thomas Grange of the *King William IV* in Fetter Lane had to appear before the licensing magistrates at the brewster sessions to account for the way he had conducted his house. The magistrates were told that three nights a week he allowed females aged sixteen upwards to meet and dance there and this had led to riotous and disorderly conduct time and time again.

The police had visited the premises unknown to the landlord and described the dancing as merely rough romping about, screaming and shouting, men pulling the women, and both stamping with such loudness that the children in the adjoining houses could not sleep. They told the magistrates that there was not open immorality but there were other disgraceful proceedings and after the parties left the

Rough romping about, screaming and shouting

dance room they all went into the drinking part of the house and indulged in liquor. They cited a couple of cases where young girls had been morally injured by the keeping up of this dancing revelry. The bench retired to consider the case and decided to withdraw Mr Grange's licence.

A few weeks later, on 12 October, Mr Grange went back to the magistrates at the Guildhall. He accused a neighbour, joiner George Appleton, of perjury saying that his false evidence of singing and dancing at the *King William* on the Monday and Tuesday nights of August race week had led to the licence being withdrawn. He produced a witness, tailor William Hammond, who said he had been there between 7 and 11 o'clock on both nights and there was no dancing going on. The landlord said there were plenty more witnesses but the magistrates refused to issue a summons and told him to apply to the court of the Queen's Bench. The *King William* remained in business until its closure in 1927.[10]

A loaded revolver
1887

At a musical evening at the *Alexandra Hotel* in Market Street on Monday 24 January a man was singing 'Time's but fleeting' and being continually annoyed by one of the guests. The culprit was Albert Haddock, a young butcher. He was staying at the hotel, and was so drunk that the landlady had refused to serve him, but she had eventually agreed to sell him two-pennyworth on condition he wet straight to bed after drinking it. It seems that John Fleming, a fitter who lived in Nunnery Lane, had objected to Albert's behaviour. Albert followed him to the door, pulled out a revolver and held it to the fitter's head saying 'I can do you bastard any time'. When PC Bainbridge arrived he found Albert in the back parlour, behaving more quietly but still very drunk. Albert at first denied having the gun, but then took it out of his pocket and said to the constable 'Take it. You can shoot me with it and then it will all be done'.

In court the next day Albert said he normally kept the revolver in his shop and had never meant to harm anyone with it. He had been having a difficult time with his wife and this had caused him to drink too much. He was sent to prison for fourteen days.

The following Monday landlord Robert Slater also had to appear in court and was fined £2 and costs for allowing drunkenness in his hotel.[11]

CHAPTER 7

A Fine Feast

A voracious fellow
1825

On a Monday December evening a crowd gathered from far and wide for an enormous meal, at the *Windmill* at Castle Mills – but only one man among them sat down to eat. A few weeks before, the rotund gentleman had enhanced his reputation by attempting to devour 10 lb of tripe at the *White Swan* in Goodramgate. The press, which compared him to a boa constrictor, reported that his stomach had failed him at the seventh pound and ended the disgusting spectacle, but this seemed only to raise the expectations of his numerous followers. He boasted he would eat a goose in less than an hour. A fine

His feat was timed at 34 minutes

goose weighing 8½ lb was spitted and served up to him, garnished with sage and onions, and his feat was timed at thirty-four minutes. A giblet pie, including the blood, was placed before him and, after consuming it with ease, he asked for 2 lb of cheese. Landlord William Vause politely declined.[1]

A Waterloo celebration at the *Black Swan*
1839

On a Tuesday evening in June a group of sergeant-majors and sergeants met in the *Black Swan* to celebrate the twenty-fourth anniversary of the Battle of Waterloo. They were from the Royal Regiment of Dragoons and the 7th (Queen's Own) Hussars, both based at the barracks. Three veterans of 18 June 1815 were present, proudly wearing their medals. It was reported that every delicacy in season was served up, reflecting great credit on the host and his wife, and that due justice was done to the quality wines. The cavalrymen enthusiastically drunk many toasts including Queen Victoria, the dowager Queen Adelaide and the rest of the royal family, the Duke of Wellington and Lord Rowland Hill who had led the Allied 1st corps in the battle.[2]

A veteran of Trafalgar
1852

A late echo of the Napoleonic wars was heard in 1852 at the *Cricketers Arms* in Tanner Row. Here the inquest was held on John Stokoe, aged about seventy, who had been a naval surgeon at the battle of Trafalgar and later one of Napoleon's personal medical attendants on the island of St Helena where the emperor was exiled until his death in 1821. John had later moved to Durham and had come to York to visit his daughter's grave. He had managed to walk to and from the cemetery but died in refreshment rooms at the railway station. The usual verdict of 'died by the visitation of God' was given. The edition of the *York Herald* reporting the inquest also carried news of the Duke of Wellington's death.[3]

A Crimean anniversary
1855

Britain's next war of significance was fought in the present-day Ukraine. The Battle of Inkerman was fought on 5 November 1854 in the misty hills of the Crimea and a year later a large party of gentlemen dined together at the *Golden Lion* in St Sampson's Square to commemorate the famous victory over the Russian forces. The press reported that the excellent dinner reflected great credit on landlord

Loyal and patriotic toasts were given

Thomas Scott and his wife. It added that the usual loyal and patriotic toasts were given with much enthusiasm and the proceedings passed with the greatest éclat.[4]

Painters, Masons and Oddfellows

While the Merchant Tailors and Merchant Adventurers of the city met in their grand halls, the painters and other such tradesmen met in the city's inns. In 1858 York's stonemasons held a series of strike meetings at the *Blue Bell* in Fossgate.

Two years later the painters held several meetings in the *Three Cranes* in St Sampson's Square to try to resolve a dispute with some of their employers. Higher wages in other towns were drawing many painters away and the local men had asked their employers for a pay rise to take their weekly wage up to 6*d*.

By the beginning of June, all but one or two employees had agreed to the increase and on Saturday evening, 1 September, forty members of the York House Painters Association spent some of their new-found wealth on dinner at the *Three Cranes*. Their toasts included the army and navy, the Guildhall, the Master Painters of York, and their host William Briggs.

The following New Year's Day William hosted the annual dinner for a hundred railway workers, and occasionally an Oddfellows lodge numbering eighty or more dined there.[5]

The Punch Bowl, *named after the Whig party's traditional drink*

The two most popular inns for large dinners were both in Stonegate,
the *Punch Bowl* which still graces the picturesque old street and the
White Hart, a white medieval building which is now a shop.

The *White Hart* was originally the *White Dog* until new landlord
Matthew Todd changed its name in about 1830, having moved there

from the *Golden Fleece*. It was already a popular venue for the Odd-fellows, the previous landlord Mr Grainger being a lodge member. In 1822 a hundred members of the Grand Provincial Lodge ended their celebrations there with several toasts and the renaissance chant *Non nobis Domine*.

When Matthew took over he completely refurbished the inn and enhanced its reputation for good food, being particularly proud of his mock turtle soup. Among his many guests were the Ancient Free Gardeners whose annual dinners were held here on Tuesday after-noons in May. When their Violet Lodge met here in 1840 they had decorated the large room with flowers and evergreens and hung banners at each end proclaiming 'Long live the Queen' and 'The Queen, God bless her'.

Matthew died in 1853 at the age of sixty-two, and for a time his widow Isaline carried on the good work. The 1858 New Year's Eve dinner for the smiths of the North Eastern Railway Company was one of her last, and shortly afterwards the inn was put up for sale. Within a couple of years it had closed.[6]

Thomas Fox was the *Punch Bowl's* landlord in the mid-nineteenth century, when the inn was at the height of its popularity. Bearing the sign of the Whig party, the inn had been a venue for political meetings and elections in the eighteenth century but now, in addition to various lodges of the Oddfellows, his guests included the Moulders' Society, friendly societies, insurance company employees and mem-bers of the United Journeymen Carriers. At the fifteenth anniversary dinner of the Baronet's Lodge of the Kingston Unity of Oddfellows, held here in 1858, it was reported that after dinner the usual loyal toasts were given, interspersed with songs amongst which were *The Farmyard*, inimitably sung by Thomas Ferrand: medieval chant had been replaced by modern music. The health of the medical officers of the lodge in the district was given with musical cheers.

It remained a popular dining place until 1880, when it was sold by Melrose to Hotham's brewery and acquired a reputation as a house of ill-repute. Happily, the *Punch Bowl* has now been restored to its former glory.[7]

A farewell supper at the *Jolly Bacchus*
1873

For a great number of years an investment club had met at the *Jolly Bacchus* beside Micklegate Bar but in February 1873 the inn was about to close. Landlord John Cooper laid on a farewell supper in the Monday evening for about thirty members and friends. The room in

The Jolly Bacchus, *named after the Roman god of wine*

which they dined had once been a watch room for the guardians of
the city before the police force was formed and was used as a deten-
tion cell for offenders. Those at the dinner drank to the health of the
landlord and his family and expressed their gratitude for his past
hospitality to their club. In May the demolition was completed,
allowing the road through Micklegate Bar to be widened.

There was a sad sequel on a Wednesday afternoon that August.
Thomas Richardson, a former landlord of the *Jolly Bacchus* who was
also a retired farmer, was walking along Micklegate with his wife to
catch a train to Harrogate. They were probably late for the train and
as he was feeling ill, he asked his wife to go on ahead to buy the
tickets. As he turned the corner into Railway Street (now George
Hudson Street) he was seen to stagger and shopkeeper Mr Cooper
brought him some brandy. Sergeant Beal sent for a surgeon but Mr
Richardson died before the surgeon arrived. The coroner's verdict
was that he died of a heart disease.[8]

CHAPTER 8

After Hours

Sunday prayers at the *Beeswing*
1851

Although Victorian licensing laws were more liberal than today, it was not permitted to open on a Sunday during the hours of divine service. One Sunday morning in April James Brownlee, landlord of the *Beeswing* on Hull Road, had opened his pub and inside a number of men employed at the gas works were drinking. From the window, James saw two policemen approaching and quickly poured the drinks away, but his customers were not so easily disposed of. There was no escape from the *Beeswing* without being seen by the eye of the law. The gas workers rushed upstairs into one of the four bedrooms, where one of them found a nightcap. He put in on and got into bed. The police had seen the men enter the pub, but when they searched it they found the other men kneeling at the bedside praying for their sick

He put on a nightcap and got into bed

friend. The story circulated around the gasworks and soon reached the Lord Mayor who publicly remarked that the police should have looked at the men more closely.[1]

At the *Wool Pack* window
1889

Police constables Alp and Blackburne were on watch at the cattle market on Sunday morning, 19 May. At about 9.30 PC Alp saw a woman go to the far window of the *Wool Pack*, take something from beneath her apron and hand it to someone inside. The woman waited, and after a few minutes something was handed back to her, which she put under her apron as the two policemen crossed the road towards her. PC Alp asked her what was under her apron and she handed him a pint tin bottle which he opened and drank from. It was freshly drawn beer. The woman gave her name as Margaret Odgers, who worked at the bar for the landlady Elizabeth Milner on cattle fair days, and on other days was employed by her as a cleaner. She asked the police to say no more about it. She told them that the previous night Mrs Milner had given her some broken meat and some beer, but she could not carry both, so she had called at the inn in the morning to collect the beer.

Mrs Milner had to appear at the Guildhall the following Wednesday accused of having kept her house open for the sale of intoxicating liquor outside permitted hours. The magistrates were told that Mrs Milner and her husband had kept the *Wool Pack* for fifteen years and since his death she had kept it for another seven years and during the whole of that time there had been no complaints against them. The case was dismissed.[2]

A door papered over
1881

It was 1.30 in the cold morning of Friday 4 February and police constables Dean and Bainbridge knocked at the door of the *Bay Horse* in Walmgate. They heard shuffling inside the inn, and footsteps running up and down stairs, and eventually the door was opened to them by the new landlord. Finding no-one downstairs, they decided to search the upstairs bedrooms. In one they found two men in bed, who gave their names as Thomas Ellis and William Hope.

In another room they found James Conlin, dressed and lying on a bedstead and mattress pretending to be asleep. They got him up and PC Dean pulled the bedstead aside, and behind it he found a door papered over. They got the door opened and found prostitutes Sarah

Ann Blessington and Mary Harrison sitting there on chairs inside a dirty lumber room.

In court the following Monday James Conlin claimed that he was in the service of the landlord and the magistrates gave him the benefit of the doubt.

Thomas Ellis told the magistrates that he had quarrelled at home and had gone to the *Bay Horse* to find a bed for the night. William Hope's only defence was that he had no home and had to lodge anywhere he could find. The magistrates fined each of them 10s.

The two women did not appear in court, nor did the landlord who was still waiting to receive his licence.[3]

Biscuits and ale
1844

On Saturday 1 June Charles Turner, keeper of the *Pheasant* beer house in New Walk Terrace, appeared before the magistrates at the castle charged with having kept his house open for the sale of beer during the hours of divine service the previous Sunday morning. Just before 11 o'clock policeman Key went into the house and found a soldier and another man there with a pitcher of ale on their table. In the back room he found three boys, aged twelve, thirteen and fourteen, who told him that the landlord had served them with biscuits and ale. The policeman reprimanded Mr Turner for serving ale to the boys but the landlord said 'If they were only five years old I would fill for them'. In court he pleaded ignorance of the law and was fined £1 with 11s costs.[4]

A quantity of copper
1834

Richard Richmond had been a servant at Dringhouses but now spent much of his time at the *Leopard* in Pavement. He was there with his brother on Wednesday 26 February. When landlord William English asked them to leave they agreed to do so and walked up the yard to the brew house to spend the next four hours with the brewer, and continued to enjoy the landlord's ale.

Next door, Mr Nelson had locked up his brazier's business for the night, but returned the following morning to find that a window had been forced open and a piece of copper which he had ready for smelting had been stolen. He put a value of about 50s on it.

The copper was found under a beam in Mr Wilkinson's hay chamber in Dringhouses, in which Richard Richmond lived. The following Tuesday he faced trial at the Guildhall and was found guilty. He was imprisoned for six months.[5]

Footprints on the stairs
1842

An inn called the *Pack Horse* had stood in Skeldergate for sixty years
or more. Behind the front door there was a passage between the bar
and the kitchen, with stairs leading up to landlord Robert Richardson's living quarters. It was in this passage, on Friday 25 February
that Michael Jackson found James Johnson sheltering from the rain.
Johnson was a native of Belfast, and had travelled to York from
London a week ago. He asked Michael Jackson where he could get a
drink of rum and Jackson directed him into the kitchen. He lit his pipe
while Mrs Richardson poured him a glass of rum, and, when he had
finished his drink, he left the kitchen and went out to leave.

Twenty minutes later Mrs Richardson went upstairs and was
surprised to find wet footprints going up to the top. In the bedrooms
all of the drawers had been ransacked. She called her husband. Mr
Richardson sent for the police and went out to help them search for
Johnson. He spotted him going into a beer house in Church Lane,
Spurriergate. The police arrested Johnson when he came out, and
found the stolen goods on him, which he told them he had bought
from a man in the street.

The next day he appeared before the magistrates, charged with
stealing a silver watch, a silver Forester's medal with a ribbon
attached, six silver teaspoons, a silver tablespoon, a brooch, two pairs
of ear drops and two silk handkerchiefs. He was committed for trial.[6]

CHAPTER 9

Adventures with Beer

A lover of the barrel
1851

Late one night in August a young man was seen by some of the household of the *Brewer's Arms* in Tanner Row climbing over a wall into the yard. He went into the privy and no further notice was taken of him until a flash of light was seen from the cellar door which had no fastening. Landlord Mr Letby was woken by his family and went to call the police. When PC Brown arrived the landlord took him into the cellar where they found the young man, Henry Dunn, intoxicated. A piece of candle and some matches were lying on the floor and a beer measure was lying on top of one of the barrels.

At the Guildhall, the court was told that Henry had previously been employed at the *Brewer's Arms* and the landlord did not wish to press charges.[1]

They found him intoxicated

A visit to the garret
1847

On the night of Wednesday 10 February Irishman Patrick Morgan was staying at William Smith's *Black Horse* in Fossgate. He awoke during the night and went up into the garret where his dreams came true – he had found three or four dozen bottles of porter. He took a handful of them back to his room, drank the contents and made two more trips before the noise awakened the landlord's son. Mr Smith junior went along to Morgan's room where he found two empty bottles on the table and some full ones hidden in the visitor's coat. Morgan said he would pay, but had no money, and was handed over to the police.[2]

He took a handful of bottles back to his room

Footprints in the cellar
1873

On a Sunday evening in October, at about 6 o'clock, William Rickell, landlord of the *Anchor* in Skeldergate, left his house after locking his cellar door which fronted onto Queen's Staith. When he returned at about 7.30 he found that the cellar door had been burst open. A twenty-four gallon beer barrel had been turned over on its side and the floor was covered with beer. There were also several footprints embedded into the newly-cemented floor.

While the landlord had been away, a labourer from Skeldergate, Patrick Boyne, had been seen with a bucket near the cellar door. He had chased away a group of children who were standing by watching him, and one of them later said he had seen Boyne in the street drinking from a bucket.

When he was arrested Boyne denied being near the *Anchor*, but the nails and edges of his boots were found to match the footprints in the cellar floor and he was sent to prison for three months.[3]

Barrels of porter
1838

On Thursday 9 August Mary Castle and Mary Emmerson were charged with stealing a great quantity of porter from Mr Potts who kept a beer house in Lady Peckitt's yard. The previous May he had bottled two large barrels of porter and now, although little had been sold, only a few bottles were left. The younger of the two, Mary Castle, worked for him and when he accused her of theft she refused to say anything until he sent for the police. She then claimed that Emmerson had taken two aprons and a handkerchief from her and would not give them back unless she stole ginger beer and porter for her. As a further incentive, Emmerson had then offered to buy her a new dress if she would steal more.

At the Guildhall Emmerson told the magistrates that she had drunk all of the porter herself, but it transpired that more than forty gallons were missing, amounting to a gallon a day. The magistrates thought she must have sold most of it. Mr Potts intervened on behalf of the two women, saying that the two days they had spent in prison before the trial were sufficient punishment and persuaded the magistrates to discharge them.[4]

The effects of half a gallon of rum
1852

One evening in September, Josiah Walker, a labourer, went into the *Ship* in Skeldergate somewhat the worse for drink. When the landlord Mr Rounding refused to serve him, Walker knocked him to the

He knocked the landlord to the ground

ground, badly cutting his face; then attacked the landlord's two daughters.

At the trial the next day, it came to light that the defendant had drunk half a gallon of rum before arriving at the *Ship*. He said he had put a water bucket into a hogshead and filled it with rum. When the judge asked him if he had drunk the whole bucket-full he admitted 'I think there must have been a drop left in it'. The judge remarked that the defendant must be suffering from 'aberrations of the mind' and fined him only 20*d*, with a further surety of 10*d* to keep the peace.[5]

A sad domestic story
1889

On Monday 13 May Ellen Taylor of Bishophill was charged with the theft of a bottle of brandy from the *Haymarket Inn*. The landlord, Mr Cox, said that she had been there the previous Wednesday when she drank three glasses of beer and was treated to more drinks by a group of men. He had missed the bottle of brandy shortly after she left. Her defence said that she was well connected and had led a reputable life until she had been taken ill some time ago. Her doctor had advised her to take beer or stout to cure her illness and this had led to her drinking to excess from time to time, causing her husband and friends a great deal of trouble. The magistrates were sympathetic and bound her over for six months.[6]

CHAPTER 10

Unwelcome Guests

A reward of 20 guineas
1809

The attention of constables and others for the apprehension of Margaret Wrightson and her paramour for taking a large sum of money from a room in the Ham & Firkin Inn in this city is particularly requested.

Advertisement – 20 guineas reward.

Whereas Margaret Wrightson of the city of York did on Thursday night last take from out of a room in the dwelling house of Mr Berry, the Ham & Firkin Inn in Walmgate, banknotes and cash amounting to £450 together with a draft note to the value of £10 together with a gold watch, single-cased, two large seals and one small one, and also several articles of linen etc. with a large square trunk with liver-coloured hair skin.

The above Margaret Wrightson is about 27 years of age, middle-sized, fair coloured and rather slender, and when she left home very much pregnant, and on Friday was last seen on the road between York and Guisbro' in a post chaise with a middle-sized man about 40 years of age and who it is supposed was assisting to take her into the neighbourhood of Guisbro' for the purpose of her laying-in.

Whosoever shall bring the said Margaret Wrightson to Mr Thomas Atkinson of Walmgate, York, shall receive a reward of 20 guineas and any person who can inform the said Thomas Atkinson of where she is shall be handsomely rewarded.[1]

The chicory grower of Coffee Yard

In 1851 Mrs Ellen Jeffrey lived with her two children, ten-year-old Anne and eight-year-old James at the *Saracen's Head*, on the corner of Stonegate and Coffee Yard. It was an old establishment having been a coffee house in the early eighteenth century. Her husband, John, had been landlord there since about 1840, but she was now widowed and, at the age of thirty-seven, ran the inn as well as looking after her children, helped by her young servant Anne Pearson. The one other member of her household, twenty-eight-year-old John Marshall, had lodged there for some time. He was once a butcher, but was now a chicory grower, the roots of which were dried and roasted for use as a coffee substitute.

On the evening of 11 July he was drunk and disorderly in the house, probably not for the first time. Ellen threatened to send for her brother, a farmer named Richardson. Marshall then threatened to kick her and she fled to take refuge two doors away in the house of Mr and Mrs Cave, an engraver and his wife, both well into their seventies. When Ellen's brother arrived at the inn, Marshall broke open a chest where the spirits were kept and helped himself to some gin. After threatening to murder Ellen he was thrown out.

At about 2 o'clock in the morning, without a bed for the night, he scaled the nine-foot wall behind the inn and threw a tile through the window of the room where his landlady was sleeping. It took three policemen to get him to the police station. That same morning he appeared at the Guildhall charged with assaulting policeman Hardy in the execution of his duty, causing a disturbance, and using threatening and abusive language. He was fined 40s with a month's hard labour in default, and bound over to keep the peace towards his landlady.

By the following year it was said that he had appeared before the bench many times and he was charged once more, this time with assaulting Ellen. He was said to have been drunk for many days and when she finally attempted to turn him out, he struck her on the left

He was charged with assaulting a policeman

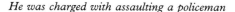

side of the head and tried to pull her cap off. He had also broken one of her windows, and the press reported that her children had been living in bodily fear of him. The magistrates fined him what they said was 'the utmost penalty' of £5.

It seemed to make little impression. The following May it was reported that John Marshall, the 'Coffee Yard offender' who had so often been charged with disorderly conduct against Mrs Jeffrey, was before the bench for having created another disturbance. On this occasion she declined to appear in court and was represented by the two policemen who had taken him into custody. The magistrates sent him to the House of Correction at Baile Hill for seven days.

However she did appear in court on the Thursday of the following week, but this time on the wrong side of the law, charged with opening her house before noon on the previous Sunday. Two policemen had gone into the *Saracen's Head* at 10.20 and found more than twenty men drinking there. Most were Hussars who claimed that they were staying at the inn and that the one or two civilians with them were their guests. The magistrates, perhaps sympathetic to her, fined her 10s instead of the customary £5.

Within two months it was John Marshall's turn to appear in court again. The press reported, in what it called a cowardly assault, that on the previous Saturday night he had entered the *Saracen's Head* and used the most coarse and insulting language towards Mrs Jeffrey, had struck her upon the head most violently, tore off her cap and nearly destroyed her dress by rough treatment. She had managed to escape and taken refuge in another room of the inn. In court she said her lodger was in the constant habit of ill-treating her and insulting her customers in every possible way, and had materially injured her business, his declared intention being to bring her to ruin and to compel her to leave the *Saracen's Head*. He had also written several scandalous letters about her and sent them to her friends.

Marshall made no attempt at defence and was sentenced to six months in the House of Correction. The magistrates told him he would be released if he could find two respectable householders who would be answerable for his future good behaviour. It seems that he was eventually able to find two people foolish enough to do so, and before the end of the year he was back in court, charged with being drunk and disorderly at the *Saracen's Head* at 11 o'clock the previous night. He was taken into custody, conducting himself in a very disreputable manner, and was sent back to the House of Correction.

Mrs Jeffrey left the *Saracen's Head* soon afterwards and in 1870 the magistrates withdrew its licence. Mr Stephenson, a wire worker, and James Hurworth, who lived opposite, complained that landlord

William Dobbey was allowing the house to be used for immoral purposes. At the brewster sessions in August the owners, Hotham & Co., told the magistrates that as soon as they had become aware of this they had given the landlord notice to quit and he was due to leave the next month.[2]

Genuine Thompson

Our first acquaintance with Robert Thompson is on a Tuesday afternoon in 1851 when he and another young man went into Miss Jane Briggs' *Crown & Anchor* in Market Street for a drink. Jane refused to serve them, probably on account of their age and our friend turned his anger on a card table, kicking it until it broke into pieces. He found himself before the magistrates in the Guildhall the following day. It was said that the value of the table was no more than 4*s* and the fragments worth 6*d*. The court made him pay damages amounting to the difference of 3*s* 6*d*, and a further 3*s* costs.

Within the next dozen years he had been in prison a good twenty times. He was known as Genuine to the locals and to the police who also described him as a 'drunken lunatic' – the press more generously called him a 'half-witted fellow'. In August 1861 he was accused of stealing money from a drunken sailor from South Shields in whose company he had been. In spite of some money being found in his

A half-witted fellow

boots, Genuine protested his innocence, although he did admit knowing where the sailor's coat was – he was remanded in custody to help find it.

Two years later, in October 1863, he went into John Beaumont's *Black Horse* in Walmgate and got himself thrown out for creating a disturbance. With no tables to kick he let rip by breaking four squares of glass for which he had to pay 5s damages and costs.

In the same year, on the Monday after Christmas he was found in a drunken state at 6 o'clock in the afternoon by PC Dickinson. Genuine's face was covered with red mud and soot, the whole of his hair was cut and a round patch shaven in the crown of his head. He said this had been done to him at Suggitt's in Pavement where the people he was with had also burned his cap. He was charged the following day with being disorderly and sent to prison for a further seven days.

Genuine had been free for only two weeks when he was in trouble once more. He now lived in North Street alongside the river, working as a brewer for James Moore of the *Black Boy*, where we have already witnessed a performance of *Hamlet*. Our friend was involved in a feud with Thomas and Margaret Smith who kept the *Blue Bell* four doors away. On the Wednesday afternoon he had broken a window at the *Blue Bell*, threatening to knock out the squares of glass as fast as they were put in, and had thrown water over Mrs Smith. Two policemen found a large crowd shouting and cheering in the street surrounding the pair. They managed to break through the circle of spectators to find Mrs Smith using disgusting language and scratching the hapless Genuine's blood-covered face. In court the following day the magistrates fined Mrs Smith half a crown, deciding that she had been the victim of extreme provocation. Genuine was given another seven days.

On Wednesday 9 March he was back in action. Mr Smith admitted to punishing him for calling Mrs Smith an objectionable name, throwing a pitcher at her and threatening to kill her. Genuine was discharged after promising to refrain from carrying out his threat. His employer's wife Agnes Moore had come to his defence against Mr Smith and in court accused the landlord of the *Blue Bell* of striking her in the face for her troubles. Ignoring the magistrates, Mr Smith and Mrs Moore began a cross-examination of each other in which neither shone to advantage. The press, probably tongue-in-cheek, reported that no damage was done to their well-known characters and the case was dismissed.

Three months later Genuine was again in trouble for throwing stones through the *Blue Bell's* window, having been ejected from the inn. At his twenty-third court appearance he was given his usual seven-day sentence.[3]

Joseph Murgatroyd

We meet Joseph Murgatroyd before the magistrates at the Guildhall on 14 May 1850, posing as an American and going under the name of Joseph Collingwood. He had already achieved notoriety and had graced many prisons with his presence.

On the previous evening, a Monday, he had gone into the *Shakespeare Tavern* close to the Minster to sample landlord William Braithwaite's rum. He then asked for something more grateful to his palate 'in the shape of teas and other good things'. Perhaps knowing of Joseph's reputation, Mr Braithwaite refused and our friend broke three squares of window glass in his usual professional style. At the trial he admitted having been in court before, but could not remember under what name. He was unwilling or unable to pay the 6*s* damages and the magistrates sentenced him to two months' hard labour.

Back in the Guildhall in 1852, on Wednesday 29 September, we find him charged with roguishly obtaining board and lodgings, with a charge of being an idle person thrown in for good measure. Having run up an unpaid bill of £1 at the *Robin Hood* (now the *Little John*) in Castlegate, he had also refused to pay for his dinner and coffee in Mrs Bowyer's eating house in Railway Street. He behaved very violently in court and was rewarded with seven more days in prison.

Three years later, on 29 November, dressed as usual in his old white hat and clothing to match, he was again before the magistrates.

He broke three squares of window glass

They were told that on the previous afternoon, a Sunday, he had walked into one of the front rooms at the *Old George* in Pavement, and coolly remarked to landlord William Bland that there was no fire. Mr Bland calmly agreed, and Joseph then asked for something to eat and drink. Recognising Joseph, probably by his attire, he remembered that he had once discussed a first rate breakfast with him at the *Old George* but for some unaccountable reason his guest had forgotten to pay. Mr Bland told Joseph he could have nothing and asked him to leave. Joseph left immediately but no sooner had he entered the street than he smashed eight panes of glass in the inn's windows, hurling a good piece of abuse at the landlord.

Mr Bland told the magistrates that he had since heard that Joseph had been staying at the nearby *Clarence Hotel* for a week and landlord Mr Hebblethwaite had still not been paid.

The magistrates fined Joseph £1 and costs which as usual he refused to pay. Well aware of his window-breaking habits, they sent him to the House of Correction for another two months' hard labour.[4]

A break-in through the privy-hole
1836

It was reported that on a Tuesday night at the beginning of March thieves got into the yard of the *Bowling Green Inn*, Lowther Street, through the opening in the privy hole. They then forced their way into the inn through the cellar door. Their haul included a quantity of gin, rum and brandy, 4 or 5 lb of cheese, 8 or 9*d* worth of tobacco, a wooden box containing small change and a pair of silver sugar tongs. So far they had escaped detection.[5]

Burglars under the bed
1848

It was 11 o'clock at night on Wednesday 3 December when Mary Kitchen, a servant at the *King's Head* in Fossgate, heard her mistress's child scream. She went upstairs to bring it down and saw that someone was under the bed. She calmly walked downstairs before raising the alarm and Mr Beetham, a painter living in Lendal, went into the bedroom where he found a man hiding under the bed with his shoes in his hands.

The following day Isaac Thompson appeared at the Guildhall accused of having been concealed in the house. In his defence he said that he had only arrived in York that night from Preston, and having no money and no place to lodge at he entered the public house and went upstairs to sleep. It was said that he had been caught coming down the stairs of the *Admiral Hawke* public house in Walmgate on the Friday night of the previous week, and he was sent to the House of Correction where he would find somewhere to sleep for the next three months.[6]

In 1880 Barnabas Marshall was landlord of the *Golden Slipper*. On a Saturday evening in November his granddaughter Miss Pratt went upstairs into her bedroom and struck a match to see her way. The match was immediately blown out and when she lit another she saw

He caught the intruder in the bedroom

someone getting under her bed. She ran downstairs to give the alarm and a customer went up to investigate. He found no-one in her room, but in a bedroom on the next floor he caught the intruder. The intruder's boots were found in another bedroom, and a coat was found which he had taken out from a drawer.

The prisoner, named as John Quinn of nearby Aldwark, appeared at the Guildhall two days later. The magistrates were told that he had been a respectable working man but had been out of work for the last few months. To get him back into the habit they sentenced him to a month's hard labour.[7]

'I don't care for all the bobbies in York'
1863

In the nineteenth century in Tanner Row, opposite the *Brewer's Arms* (which became *Flares* in 2002) there stood an inn named after Sir Sydney Smith, a British Admiral. Landlord James Lowe ran the inn in the 1840s and 1850s and renamed it the *Sun*. In about 1860 William Morrell took over.

On a Saturday evening in August of that year two hawkers arrived at his inn. William served each of them with a glass of wine, and then showed them upstairs to a double-bedded room where they could lodge for the night. He left them to unpack, but when he returned a few minutes later he found one of them, James McGrath, at his bedroom door. The suspicious landlord went back down and listened at the foot of the stairs. Hearing footsteps going into his bedroom he returned and caught McGrath in the room, trying to open the box in which he kept his money. He asked what McGrath was doing and the hawker answered 'What the devil is that to you?'. William threatened to call the police, to which McGrath said 'I don't care for all the bobbies in York' and ran back into his own room, barricading the door with furniture. A policeman broke open the door and took the hawker into custody.

At the Guildhall the following Monday, James McGrath's defence said that he was a respectable man who was in the habit of attending fairs as a hawker and had forty stones of filberts waiting for him at the railway station. He was not a likely person to take advantage by robbery of anyone. Policeman Kinson also spoke in his defence, saying that he had known him for four years, although a subsequent witness claimed the defendant was an accomplice of card sharps. The character references were enough to convince the magistrates to give him the benefit of the doubt and he was discharged.[8]

Burglary at the *Mason's Arms*
1864

William Storey and his family were awakened in the early hours of Friday 29 July by the sound of breaking glass. William, landlord of the *Mason's Arms* in Fishergate, looked out of the bedroom window of the inn but saw no-one. Searching the house he found that another window, overlooking an adjoining urinal, had been broken, but could see no-one outside. He then found a coat, a hat and a boot. It seemed that a burglar had been disturbed by the family awakening and had beaten a hasty retreat leaving some clothes behind.

Shortly before 4 o'clock that morning, a policeman was walking his beat at the top of Blue Bridge Lane when he met a man without boots and without a hat and coat. Knowing a burglar when he saw one, he took the suspect along to the lock-up where he was kept in custody until he could be brought before the magistrates. It was learned that the items of clothing found by the landlord belonged to the prisoner and the police noticed a number of bruises on him, thought to have been sustained when he dropped from the window at the inn. He gave his name as Cornelius Kempster, and said he was a fitter from Waterloo Road in London.

He was charged with burglary, along with Michael Boland, an Irish labourer. They had been living at Pitt's lodging house in Walmgate and a servant there gave evidence that neither of them were in the house at the time of the robbery. Boland was released with no firm evidence against him but Kempster was committed for trial.[9]

The curious case of the wellington boots
1850

In 1850 the local press reported a curious sequence of burglaries from public houses. It began in March at the *Leopard* in the Shambles, with a series of break-ins through the cellar grate. The thief had taken a large amount of ale, beef, mutton and coal, and also helped himself to a pair of wellington boots. Landlord Davidson said he had his suspicions as to who was responsible.

On Thursday 17 May there was a break-in at the *Lion & Lamb* in Blossom Street through an unfastened window. The only item taken from landlord John Brown was a pair of wellingtons.

The following week the victim was landlord Thomas Nicholson. As a twenty-five-year-old sergeant-major, Thomas had suffered a sabre-wound from a French cavalryman at Waterloo and had been discharged from the army the following year. He had taken over the *Light Horseman*, close to Fulford cavalry barracks, some twenty-five years later. On the Sunday night of 20 May thieves removed a pane of glass from his kitchen window and took away with them two hams, three German silver teaspoons and salt and mustard spoons engraved with the initials TJN. They also took Thomas's shooting jacket and his wellingtons. Sadly Thomas died four months later, at the age of sixty.[10]

A night on the tiles
1874

Landlord David Rennison of the *Yorkshireman* in Coppergate went into his yard at 10 o'clock on a June Saturday evening and spotted a man on the sloping roof of one of the inn's outhouses. He shouted 'Holloa, what are you doing there?', but there was no reply. The landlord called for the police, and when the policeman arrived the intruder came down claiming he had been looking for his hat. He then excused himself and walked away.

The policeman noticed that, above the section of roof, in the main building there was an open window. It was the bedroom of one of the servants, and going up to check she found the bedclothes thrown off, her box emptied and the contents of the drawers strewn all over the floor. The only item missing seemed to be her alpaca umbrella.

The intruder was identified as Benjamin Wrigglesworth, a labourer. In court he admitted that he might have had a drop of beer on the Saturday night and been on top of the tiles but he denied having been in the servant's room. He was remanded for a week, then convicted of being 'a rogue and a vagabond' and sent to prison for a month.[11]

'Where did you keep the whisky?'
1896

At about 6 o'clock on the Tuesday morning of 14 January in *St Leonard's Club*, steward Henry Smith opened his bedroom door. On a window ledge on the staircase he noticed a pair of shoes and a cap. The window had been taken out and was resting against the ledge. Downstairs the place was in uproar. Articles were strewn all over the floor including a coat which none of the servants could identify, and a three-quarters smoked cigarette was found in one of the cupboards.

Detective Sergeant Alp was sent to the scene and concluded that the thief had climbed over the garden fence behind the club leading to the roof. He traced the footprints round to the staircase window where he found the catch had been forced. He recognised the cap and coat as belonging to twenty-three-year-old Daniel Seeley, a tailor of no fixed abode. By an incredible stroke of luck the policeman had seen him in a lodging house in Rosemary Place only the previous lunchtime and, knowing of his reputation, had called him aside and quietly advised him to leave the city. Seeley had been wearing the same cap and coat. Alp informed the Chief Constable who immediately issued a description of the wanted man, who was found and arrested by PC Metcalfe.

The same day he appeared before the Lord Mayor and magistrates. He was charged with stealing 11*s*, two coats, a pair of boots, some cigars and six postage stamps, having entered the building between midnight and 6 o'clock in the morning. He replied 'I got in between twelve and two. They would not have caught me only I was drunk.'

Henry Smith was called to give evidence. He said he had gone to bed just before midnight after fastening the large window on the first flight of the main staircase.

'You left the window wide open,' Seeley interrupted to the court's amusement. 'You ought to have put a bill outside to invite people to come in.' The steward admitted that one of the catches was broken and the other did not fasten very well, so the window had to be propped shut. Seeley told him 'You said you locked everything up'.

The steward then described what he had found and held up the coat to show the court. 'That's my coat!' shouted Seeley. Smith said that in the coat pockets they had found some cigars which he could identify as they bore the club's mark.

'Where did you keep the whisky?' Seeley asked him. 'I couldn't get any whisky.' Again there was laughter from the spectators.

Trying to ignore the prisoner, Smith went on to say that between the tables in the club dining room he found the glass money box he used for the card money and a sum of 11s was missing from it. He had also noticed that glass had been removed from a skylight and placed on the roof. About twenty feet below, in the passage-way, was a large hard lump of putty. The prosecutor Mr Dale inferred that the burglar had dropped the putty to gauge how far he would have to fall, and had then decided it would be safer to use the staircase window.

The clerk to the magistrates asked whether there were any more questions. Seeley said he had already asked where the whisky was kept, and added that anyone could get into *St Leonard's Club*. 'Well somebody did,' the clerk said. The court roared with laughter as Seeley told him 'Yes, and there was nothing to get.'

The clerk said 'Do you want to ask him anything else?'

Seeley – 'Yes, I'll ask him if he fastened that window'. The embarrassed steward replied that he had and Seeley retorted 'If he had kept it fastened properly I should not have got into the club and I should not have been there. I had no tools to force the catch.'

The Lord Mayor intervened 'How did you get the pane of glass out?'

Seeley – 'I pulled it out.'

The Lord Mayor – 'That would not be a very easy matter.'

Seeley – 'Why anyone can pull one out. If you got on top of that there roof you could pull one out yourself.' (laughter)

John Buttery, the club's waiter, identified one of the stolen coats as his property. A small amount of material had been cut from around the bottom of the coat.

Seeley – 'It will just about fit him now. It was too big for him before.' (laughter)

There was no more evidence to be given or needed. The Lord Mayor said 'The bench think great credit is due to Alp and Metcalfe' and they committed the prisoner to trial at the next assizes. Seeley was also charged with two other burglaries of the clothing which he was found to be wearing.[12]

CHAPTER 11

Ladies of the Night

A prostitute robbed of her clothes
1866

Seventeen-year-old Sarah Ann Warnby had come to York from Ashton-under-Lyne. After two months of desperately trying to find employment she went to stay in William Burke's beer house in Cross Alley, off the Water Lanes, to work as a prostitute.

Between 2 and 3 o'clock on a Monday morning in February a man named Moore came in and bought a good deal of beer. As he was paying, some money fell out of his pocket and Sarah picked up two sovereigns and put them in her pocket. The landlord asked her what she had and she answered 'Nothing'. Moore eventually fell asleep and Burke asked Sarah to put her hand in the customer's pocket. She

She managed to borrow a dress

refused, but held Moore's hand up while Burke put his hand in the pocket and took out some sovereigns, half sovereigns and silver. He kept some of it and put the rest back.

Sarah was in great need of clothing, and within a day or two she had spent the two sovereigns she had picked up. On the Tuesday evening she was at a neighbour's house wearing her new clothes when Burke came in. He dragged her back to his house where he forced her to take off all of the clothes she had bought, pulled off her boots and left her wearing only an undergarment. She managed to borrow a dress from a friend and went to the police. PC Whitwell called at the house and persuaded Burke to give the clothing back to Sarah.

The case came to court on the Thursday and Burke was charged with having stolen a pair of boots, a crinoline, a shawl, a bonnet, a skirt and a gown.

There was also another charge against Burke. On the Saturday before Moore's visit, between 9 and 10 o'clock in the evening, another of his ladies, Catherine Howard, brought a man into the house. He remained there until 11.30 and Burke asked Catherine to rob him. When she refused Burke dragged her out of the house and told her he would not have her working there unless she robbed her clients for him. He then knocked her down and kicked her, breaking three of her ribs and severely injuring her foot, and badly bruising her right arm.

In court she said Burke had treated her like a dog. The Lord Mayor told Burke his conduct was the most disgraceful and wicked he had heard of and sent him to the House of Correction for six months for felony and a further six months for assault. He told the young Sarah that he hoped she had learned a salutary lesson.[1]

As deaf as a post
1833

On a Saturday afternoon in January at about 4.30, George Thompson, a farmer's servant from Raskelf, described as 'rather beyond middle age and as deaf as a post', went into the *Black Boy* in First Water Lane.

There he met two twenty-year-old ladies, Elizabeth Clark and Mary Smith. He called for a pint of ale while one of them sat on his knee and the other began to grope around his pockets. They stayed with him for only about ten minutes, and as soon as they had left he realised that his purse and watch were both missing. There had been 10s in his purse when he had put it back into his breeches after paying for his ale.

He left to follow the two girls and they were soon arrested. No money was found on them but they were sent for trial charged with

She began to grope around his pockets

committing robbery in a brothel. Both were discharged with cautions.[2]

At Mrs Megginson's

The River Ouse was the commercial life blood of the Roman, Viking and medieval city but by the mid-nineteenth century it had spawned

There was no worse house in the city

poverty and crime in the nearby streets and alleys. The King's Staith and the Water Lanes leading from the riverside to the city's streets were a web of squalid inns and beer houses, the lairs of thieves and prostitutes to entrap the unsuspecting traveller. In the 1850s and 1860s the worst of these was an infamous beer house on King's Staith run by Mrs Mary Megginson.

We are first privileged to visit her house on the night of 19

December 1854 in the company of police Sergeant Mountain. At 11.20 he went in and found nine men and ten women, all of whom were said to be well-known thieves and prostitutes. He and policemen Bagley and Farndale told the court the following Thursday that the house was 'very indifferently conducted'. The court agreed that there was no worse house in the city and the Lord Mayor commented that he could bear testimony as to the very disorderly manner in which the business was conducted in the defendant's house, which he often had occasion to pass. Mrs Megginson replied that she tried to keep it as respectable as she could, considering its bad location, but the Lord Mayor took the view that she must have known that her guests were of notoriously bad character. He fined her £2 and told her that if she appeared before him a second time the fine would be £5.[3]

An infantryman's wages
1855

One Tuesday night the following October, Private John Roxburgh of the 2nd West York Light Infantry had the misfortune to call at Mrs Megginson's with another soldier, John McConnor. Earlier that day he had received his £1 17s 6d pay. The pair went into the beer house between 10 and 11 o'clock and met privates William Heslop and Reuben Reed of the same regiment. To celebrate pay-day Private Roxburgh treated them both to three or four quarts of ale and a cigar each. He then decided we would like a gill of gin and, as Mrs Megginson was licensed only to serve beer, the four of them went to the *Ship Inn* a couple of doors away. It was Roxburgh's turn to pay again. He offered a sovereign for the gin and placed the 19s change into his pocket. Private Reed stood near to him and watched closely.

On the way back to Mrs Megginson's, Heslop came up behind Roxburgh seizing him by the throat and forcing his knee into Roxburgh's back. While Roxburgh was being held, Reed took all of the money out of their victim's trouser pocket and also a snuff box, then they knocked him down and kicked him in the ribs. John McConnor, seeing that there were friends of the two attackers keeping an eye on the situation, decided discretion was the better part of valour and ran for help. Roxburgh got to his feet and staggered back into the *Ship* with his head bleeding, followed soon afterwards by his two attackers. He accused them of robbing him but they warned him that, if he reported them, they would murder him.

The next day Roxburgh informed his sergeant major of the incident and the two were delivered into the hands of the police with a message from Major Stranbenzee expressing a wish that the matter be laid before the magistrates. In court the next Monday McConnor posit-

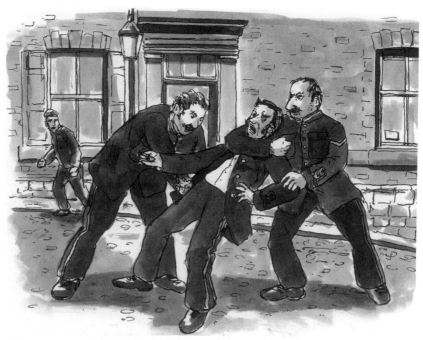

He took all of the money out of his pocket

ively identified the prisoners as the guilty men and the Lord Mayor committed them to the assizes. Hearing the verdict, Heslop immediately rushed at McConnor and punched him in the face knocking him down on top of the press reporters and continued the attack until he was restrained by a policeman.[4]

A waterman's purse
1857

On a Saturday night, 26 October 1857, Samuel Bates, a waterman from Lincoln, was in Mrs Megginson's where he met Mary Kilgarry and Mary Ann Lockett. They took him to a house round the corner in Middle Water Lane, but before he got into bed with Mary Kilgarry he hid his purse containing three sovereigns in one of his boots. She soon found it, so to keep it safe he put it into his trouser pocket and placed the trousers under the pillow under his head. After she had left him, he woke up to discover that the purse was missing and he informed the police. On the Sunday night the police came to arrest her and found her in bed with Alfred Bethany, who had the stolen purse in his possession.

He placed the trousers under his pillow

Bethany and the two women appeared in court the next day. The magistrates thought that there were doubts about the case and discharged all three.[5]

Jack ashore
1858

Sailor William Fox from Ramsgate arrived by rail in York on Wednesday evening, 17 January, and found his way to a public house on King's Staith. There he met Mary Ann White and asked her where he could find lodgings. She invited him to the house where she lived, and before they left the inn he showed his appreciation by treating her liberally to brandy, beer, oranges and oysters. They left at 10.30 to go to her house and on the way he called into a shop to buy some meat for their supper. The shopkeeper, who probably knew Mary Ann and her business, suggested that they should have a quart of ale for their supper and Fox also paid for this. They later sent for three or four half pints of gin and did not go to bed until the early hours of the morning.

Thinking her guest had fallen asleep, Mary Ann crept into his bedroom and began to search his trousers. He leapt out of bed, accusing her of robbing him, and chased her downstairs and out of the house.

Appearing in court at the Guildhall the following day, Mary Ann denied the charge and said they were drunk together. It was by no means the first time she had faced a similar charge and the Lord Mayor gave them both some good advice, after which they left the hall.

Two months later, on Saturday afternoon 27 March, John Grey, a recruit from Sheffield was drunk at Mrs Megginson's. He went upstairs with Harriet Page and when they reached the top of the staircase a man hit him on the head, knocking him down. The young recruit had Harriet arrested, accusing her of stealing three half-crowns and a sixpence from him. The next Monday they were in court, but he could not identify her positively and she was discharged.

Shortly after mid-day the following Saturday, Police Inspector Halley and Sergeant Hudson visited the house. They found five prostitutes there, with six or seven men of bad character. In court, Mrs Megginson said they had gone there for refreshment after having been to see the execution of Shepherd, a murderer. The Lord Mayor dismissed the case and warned her to be more careful in future.[6]

A hundred times worse than the rest
1869

Eleven years had passed and at the annual brewster sessions held in August the licensing magistrates were reminded of three beer houses in the Water Lanes repeatedly complained of by the police for harbouring thieves, prostitutes and other bad characters. One of these houses was Mrs Megginson's and they were told it was a hundred times worse than the others. Although repeatedly cautioned she had never taken the slightest notice and finally, after fifteen years on the edge of the law, her licence was withdrawn.

The second of these houses was *The Harp* in Middle Water Lane (now Cumberland Street), kept by William Ormesby. It was stated that his house was the resort of travelling thieves but Inspector Shields said he had never seen any prostitutes there. Some of the principal inhabitants of the parish testified to the orderly and respectable manner in which the house had been conducted and his licence was allowed to continue.

The third was the *Shoulder of Mutton* also in Middle Water Lane. Originally it held a spirit license but this had been taken away and it was now only a beer house. It was kept by Mr Smith who told the magistrates he did his best to keep disorderly customers out. The

They found prostitutes there every time

police reminded the honourable gentlemen that the landlord had
been convicted three times and they had visited the house twenty-five
times during the past year and found prostitutes there every time. An
application was made to transfer the licence to Cuthbert Thompson,
foreman of the brewery. This had been signed by the churchwardens
who probably felt that it was better for prostitution to be carried on in
a place where the police could keep an eye on it. The chief constable
supported them saying he had known the house for fourteen years
and it was impossible to prevent the assemblage of prostitutes in it.

George Gill

We meet George Gill for the first time shortly before 9 o'clock on an August evening in 1843 during a visit from Mary Doughty of Garden Place to his beer house in Church Lane off Spurriergate. She forced her way into the house and complained to him that her husband Thomas was living there with another woman. She tried to get into one of the rooms, but George pushed her back out into the lane and threw a can of water over her. She tried to open the door to get back in when he came out still holding the can and hit her across the forehead with it.

Mr Marshall, the surgeon at the police station, was called and found her with her forehead cut to the bone and her face covered in blood. He said that the blow must have been a very severe one and she seemed very sick and faint. George was fined 20s and the magistrates warned him to keep a more orderly house.

At about 8 o'clock on Sunday evening of 7 April the following year George had another visitor. Inspector Bellerby was aware of the way George's house was being conducted and listened at the door, no doubt severely shocked by the obscene language he heard. He found eight men and three prostitutes inside drinking ale. The court heard that the maximum fine was £5 but the magistrates fined him 40s. They added that that they could not shut their eyes to the fact that his house was of a very disreputable character.[7]

A tippler's revenge
1851

By 1848 George had moved to the *Ploughboy's Rest* beer house in Swinegate. The following year the police were called when a woman called Nicholls was arrested for stealing a pair of earrings which were being offered for sale there by a Jewish gentleman. George and his wife were also arrested for obstructing the police.

Two years later George was in court again, charged with keeping the *Ploughboy's Rest* open between 10 o'clock and 12 noon on Sunday 20 April. William Frederick Musham of Middle Water Lane went there at 10 o'clock in the morning and called for a pint of ale and after drinking it he had three gill bottles filled. About an hour later he went back to get another pint of ale. Mr Pratt appeared in court to represent the landlord. The local press reported his questioning of William Musham:

> Mr Pratt – 'I suppose after drinking the ale you were so filled with pious horror and indignation that you went down to the police office and gave information.'

Musham – 'No.'

Mr Pratt – 'When did you go?'

Musham – 'It was at night between nine and 10 o'clock. I was once or twice at the defendant's in the afternoon and during the night.'

Mr Pratt – 'You went in liquor to lay the information?'

Musham – 'I was in liquor certainly but I was not to call tipsy.'

Mr Pratt – 'How many pints can you drink on a reasonable calculation without being tipsy?'

Musham – 'I cannot tell.'

Mr Pratt – 'Upon your oath did you not go at 5 o'clock in the afternoon, take up somebody's measure of glass, and drink it?' (laughter)

Musham – 'Not that I know of.'

Mr Pratt – 'Did you not leave Gill's house declaring you would be revenged upon him because you had been struck there?'

Musham – 'Yes I did.'

Mr Pratt – 'Have you since expressed your regret at your having done so?'

Musham – 'Yes I have.'

Mr Pratt – 'Have you not said that the charge was a false charge?'

Musham – 'Oh no, I said I was very sorry at making the charge.'

Mr Pratt – 'Do you expect a situation in the police force?' (laughter)

Musham – 'I don't understand you.'

Mr Pratt's line of questioning then became clear. Musham had gone into the *Ploughboy's Rest* at 5 o'clock on the Sunday afternoon and drunk another man's glass of ale.

The other man struck him and

He drank another man's beer

Musham left to fetch John Smith, with whom the magistrates were well acquainted. To avoid further trouble George Gill treated Musham's notorious friend to a glass of ale and a pipe of tobacco. Smith left happily leaving Musham to the mercy of the landlord. It was then that Musham vowed revenge and made a drunken report. The magistrates felt it was impossible to convict George on this evidence and dismissed the case.

The next week a lodger at the *Ploughboy's Rest*, Harriet Stephenson, appeared in the same courtroom accused of stealing a cashmere shawl. On the Monday afternoon Mrs Gill discovered that the shawl was missing and later found Harriet wearing it. Harriet said she had borrowed the shawl to go to the theatre and had planned to return it. The case was adjourned for two days and in the meantime George withdrew the charge.[8]

Cries of murder
1851

Late into the night on a Thursday in October of the same year, neighbours reported hearing screams from inside the *Ploughboy's Rest*. Henry Hoare, a groom whose house was separated from the *Ploughboy's Rest* by a passage, heard a woman's cries of murder. He could not say whose voice it was as there were other women in the house apart from Mrs Gill. It was later said that the *Ploughboy's Rest* was a disgrace to the city and the haunt of thieves and prostitutes and strolling vagabonds and we can suspect that such noises at night were not uncommon. Mr Hoare said Mrs Gill was given to drink and quite riotous when in liquor.

Sarah Dickens was more explicit. She said that about 1.30 in the morning she heard Mrs Gill screaming loudly and Mr Gill say 'Damn you, why don't you get out?' and again 'Get out with you'. She heard Mrs Gill crying out but she heard nothing like blows. She said she had heard quarrelling several times but had never seen Mr Gill ill-treat her. Elizabeth Samuel, who lived next door but one, also heard cries of 'Murder' and claimed it was Mrs Gill's voice.

The inquest on Mrs Gill's death was held the next Saturday morning at the *Blacksmith's Arms*, Church Street. It was alleged by the neighbours that her husband had been responsible. Thomas Nicholls, Mrs Gill's brother, of nearby Coppergate said she was aged forty. He had visited her every day since Tuesday – she said she was suffering from inflammations to her body but did not speak of any blows. The post mortem had shown no signs of violence but an inflammation of the lungs and disease of the heart, brain and kidneys, the lungs from cold but the rest probably from intemperate habits, and that verdict was given.

The next April George was charged with serving drinks early on a Sunday morning. Again it was not proven but George was warned as he had already been convicted of a similar offence.

George's brushes with the law continued and in September 1855, one of the ladies in his house, Ann Jones, was charged with stealing a purse containing 10s. William Deighton, a carrier from Coxwold, had been enjoying a glass of ale in her company for about half an hour, and when he left he realised his purse was missing. The magistrates, thinking that he should have known better than to drink in such a place, dismissed the charge.

The law caught up with George in March 1857. An alpaca coat valued at 7*s* had been stolen from Mr Stowe Sharpe, a pawnbroker in Colliergate. It was found in a box at the *Ploughboy's Rest*. In court on the Saturday, George claimed he had wrapped it up by mistake when buying some other articles and would pay for it. He added that he had already been in prison since Thursday on the charge. The Lord Mayor said he would have to stay for three months longer.[9]

In the *Palace*

Close to the *Ploughboy's Rest* in Swinegate was an inn called the *Lord Nelson*. On a Saturday afternoon towards the end of August 1851 the house was full of disorderly people and some were thrown out into Swinegate where they continued fighting. PC Cooper saw William Hall strip himself in the street to join in the melee and arrested him. The policeman said that the disturbance would have lasted well into the night if he had not taken someone into custody, but asked the magistrates to be lenient towards Hall as there had been several people behaving much worse. They imposed a fine of 5*s* but in the meantime landlord Mr Carr was one of seven landlords summoned to appear at the brewster sessions. He was the only one who failed to show up and his licence was withheld.

Henry Thornton took over the *Lord Nelson* in 1854, three years after the Great Exhibition in London, and changed its name to the *Crystal Palace*. The grandiose name did nothing to enhance the reputation of the house. The police knocked at his door at 1 o'clock in the morning on Sunday 23 April and found half a dozen people drinking there. Mr Thornton said they were his friends and were celebrating the opening of his premises as a dram shop the previous day. He said he had stopped selling drinks before 12.30, and they had stayed round the fire while he supplied them with free drinks. The magistrates believed him.

Henry Thornton continued to hold the licence although by the following year the *Crystal Palace* was taken over by Henry Kilby. There were complaints at the brewster sessions that singing sessions were being held there. Mr Kilby explained to the magistrates that the concert room still belonged to Mr Thornton who let it and he had no control over the passage between the room and the public house. The magistrates told him that music rooms in the city had a demoralising effect and if it continued the licence would be under threat.

At the 1856 brewster sessions Mr Kilby was again before the magistrates, who had finally had enough and decided to withhold the licence. The Lord Mayor said the house was being kept open very late and was a resort for bad characters. A Mr Chadwick expressed his opinion, held by many, that such houses as the *Crystal Palace*, where singing rooms are carried on created ruin to the youths who were induced to visit them.

With Mr Kilby gone, it was Henry Thornton's turn once more to face the music. On a Thursday evening the next February, Inspector Haley paid him a call and found a man singing on the stage and twelve prostitutes in a room upstairs. When he brought this to Mr Thornton's attention the landlord replied that if it had been half an hour sooner he would have found twice twelve. He then said he had misheard the inspector's remark and denied that the ladies in his house were prostitutes. He complained that the other houses were allowed to harbour such characters and that it was hard that he, who tried to keep his house respectable shutting it every night at 11.00 and not opening it on Sundays, should be picked on by the police. In court a week later he was fined 10s and costs, and immediately had another charge set before him – one of obstructing the paving flags outside his shop in Church Street with a table and other furniture. He had already been cautioned for placing them there for sale, but he said that the items had already been sold and were placed there for removal. He was fined a further 5s and costs.[10]

Pawning a silver watch
1858

By March of the following year William Lazenby was landlord here and involved in the case of a silver Geneva watch said to have been stolen from him. Margaret Buck, one of the ladies lodging with him, had met a young recruit named Francis Walker at the nearby *Hand & Heart*. She took him back to the *Crystal Palace* and persuaded him to pledge his watch to the landlord for 5s to go on a drinking spree.

He pledged his watch to the landlord

Mr Lazenby later gave it back to her, expecting the young recruit to arrive shortly to redeem it, but by the time he turned up she had pledged the watch elsewhere for another 15s. The magistrates, no doubt suspicious of how the 5s had been spent, decided there was no case to answer.

Allowing bad characters to be served

The following week Mr Lazenby was fined 10*s* for allowing bad characters to assemble in his house, and again a month later when the fine was 40*s*.

On the last occasion police sergeant Mountain visited the *Crystal Palace* at 5 o'clock on a Sunday morning and knocked on the door. It was opened by the landlord and the sergeant went to look upstairs where he found two prostitutes in bed with men. The press did not report whether Margaret was one of the two.[11]

The sawdust parlour

Close to the *Crystal Palace*, on the corner of Swinegate and Grape Lane, was a public house known locally as the 'sawdust parlour'. At the time of the Napoleonic wars it was *The Rifleman*, then *The Sharp-shooter* in the 1820s. By 1841 it had become *The Bloomsbury*, named after the Bloomsbury Volunteers, a regiment made up mainly of lawyers. Most of the time, however, this inn was on the wrong side of the law. Landlord Peter Worthy put in regular court appearances for opening during the hours of divine service and allowing bad characters to be served there.

In 1857 it became *The Flying Dutchman*, and George Donaldson the new landlord soon followed his predecessor into court. On his first offence, in January 1858, he claimed that he had erred unwittingly and promised the bench that his house would be better conducted in future.

He managed to keep hold of his licence until August 1860, but in the previous December there was an incident in the house that generated some interest. It was on a Saturday evening at 9 o'clock when Robert Harrison went in and sat down next to a barber and a lace-weaver, twenty-eight-year-old Thomas Liddell and twenty-five-year-old Edward Carney. After a short while, Carney asked Harrison to drink with them, which he did, buying each of them a quart of ale in return and paying from his purse. Shortly after, he felt in his pocket for his purse and realised it was missing. He accused Liddell, who was sitting next to him, of stealing it. Liddell denied it, crossing his arms and slyly handing the purse to Carney who left hurriedly. Liddell tried to follow but was prevented from leaving and arrested. The same night Carney was arrested and although the purse was not found they were both sentenced to two years. There was considerable interest in the case because Carney was also a well-known pugilist and had recently been matched against a man from Middlesbrough in a fight due to take place the following February.

By 1869 *The Flying Dutchman* had been relegated to the status of a beer house. It was still regularly harbouring bad characters and landlady Mary Ann Long's license was withdrawn.[12]

The *Horse & Jockey*

Our next port of call in these back streets is at the *Horse & Jockey* in Little Stonegate. In the 1840s landlady Mrs Dimmock rivalled her neighbour at *The Bloomsbury* in court appearances. She left York in 1849 to marry, leaving her son in charge to follow in her footsteps.

At the 1856 brewster sessions Mr Anderson spoke of the very bad character of the house saying it was little better than a house of ill-fame. At the sessions, magistrate Mr Wilson said to Mr Dimmock 'Do you know that one house if not both on either side of the *Horse & Jockey* are emptying owing to your disorderly management?' The landlord told the magistrates 'We are told it is owing to the Banters opposite (laughter). They are a nuisance to our house for on Sunday last, the camp meeting day, they fetched water by buckets full, yes they did' (laughter).

By 1872 the house had become *The Shakespeare* and the new landlady, Margaret Dinnie, was keeping up appearances in court. At the Guildhall Mr Haley said of *The Shakespeare* 'During the time that Mrs Dinnie has been in possession of it as landlady it has been no better than the worst brothel we have had in the city. I have reports in writing about it and a petition put up by the neighbours to say that the house is a most abominable place and not at all fit to be kept as a beer house'. Lithographer Mr Monkhouse of Little Stonegate said the house was a disgrace to the whole city and for a number of years past had been the resort of the lowest of characters from different parts of the city and was not used by the neighbours for purchasing of beer. Mr Bruce, keeper of the Primitive Methodist chapel, said that for the last thirteen years it had been a convenience for the lowest classes and the neighbourhood had been greatly annoyed at the extent of the scum of the town who visited it. It was only on Tuesday last that the whole neighbourhood had been disturbed by Mrs Dinnie's drunken conduct in her own house. The magistrates transferred the licence out of her hands.[13]

The curse of the land

Close to the end of Fossgate, near Pavement, ran Black Horse Passage, leading to Wesley Place. Here in the nineteenth century there was a beer house which we have already visited in 1842 when a servant set fire to her clothes.

Some twelve years later landlord Newland Hardcastle was fined 5*s* for being drunk and disorderly. The magistrates pronounced that beer houses were the curse of the land and they were likely to be rendered greater curses still if those who conducted them were no better than the defendant.

Landlord Hardcastle was succeeded by David Dixon who was also regularly at odds with the law. Sometime after 1 o'clock on Sunday morning, 20 February 1859, Sergeant Ingram knocked at his door. The sergeant reported that the landlord answered the door 'in his shirt as though he had come down from bed'. He refused three times to allow his house to be searched on the principle that every man's home is his castle but the magistrates replied that it was already proved that the house was a report of thieves and prostitutes and that was authority enough. They fined him 5*s*.

Six weeks later, on the Sunday shortly after midnight, Sergeant George Sykes managed to gain entry to the beer house. He found fifteen men of bad character in the house all drinking ale. The following year a Mrs Coulson reported that her husband had been robbed of £10 worth of banknotes and £3 10*s* in gold while drinking there on Thursday night 17 December.

By 1866 widow Elizabeth Beaumont had taken over the house. Two policemen visited her on the Tuesday night of 6 March and found two women there of notoriously bad character. On being warned, the landlady said she could not earn a living without them. On a later visit by the police the same evening the two were still there and Mrs Beaumont, for her first offence, was fined 10*s*.

On the evening of the day of the hearing, PC Verity was walking down Black Horse Passage when Mrs Beaumont came out and abused him and called him a liar. He told the court that he had no doubt that Mrs Beaumont would have struck him had it not been for the intervention of her daughter and some of her customers. A man who described himself as a hurdy-gurdy grinder employed in her house came to her defence saying that she had tried to protect the policeman from other people in her house, but the magistrates fined her another 5s.

Seven months later Mrs Beaumont was in court again, accusing labourer Michael Kelly of stealing three gold rings from her. On a Tuesday evening she and her daughter were drinking ale in the beer house with two young men from the country. As the house was not licensed for spirits they sent out for some whisky and then went out together down the street and into Walmgate. After visiting a couple more drinking houses the men left Mrs Beaumont and her daughter and went their own way. Michael Kelly had also been drinking in the *Black Horse* beer house and had followed the group. Now that the men had left, he walked up beside the two women and accompanied them back to Fossgate. Suddenly he took Mrs Beaumont by the hand, pretending to wish her goodbye, pulled the three rings off her and ran away down Straker's Passage.

The court committed Michael Kelly for trial but took heed of the defence's statement that Mrs Beaumont was not a respectable woman and was so drunk at the time that she did not know what had happened to her rings. She was then charged with keeping her house open after midnight on the Friday, when Sergeant Ingram had found several men drinking with two prostitutes. She was fined £2 with the threat of two months' prison in default of payment.[14]

CHAPTER 12

The Old Coaching Inns

A stolen horse at the *Red Lion*
1829

On Saturday 14 November, John Dawson, from the Lincolnshire village of Metheringham, appeared at the Guildhall, charged with having stolen a black horse in his home county. Dawson had been offering the horse for sale in York market, asking a price of £14, and a man named Lister offered him £4. Possibly suspicious at Dawson's willingness to accept the low price, Lister asked him to take the horse to the *Red Lion* in Walmgate and in the meantime he reported the matter to the police. Dawson was arrested and kept in custody in the watch house in Walmgate, from where he unsuccessfully tried to escape through a chimney. He and his accomplice, William Peniston, were eventually sentenced to be transported for life.

There is a legend that the more famous horse thief Dick Turpin had attempted to escape the clutches of the law by way of a chimney at the *Red Lion* and it seems likely that the tale was based on Dawson's escapades.[1]

Two guineas reward
1820

Whereas some evil-disposed person or persons did on Monday night last wilfully and maliciously cut the horses' harnesses from the coach which runs from York to Selby belonging to Mr J Benson while standing opposite the Wheat Sheaf Inn in Castlegate.

Notice is hereby given that whoever will give information of the offender or offenders to Mr John Cartwright of the Wheat Sheaf Inn aforesaid so that they may be brought to justice shall receive two guineas reward from the said John Cartwright.[2]

The coaching era was more than 150 years old but only in the last few years had road improvements led to faster coaches being built. Faster travel meant cheaper travel, with fewer stops for meals and sleep. The journey between York and London had been cut from four days to just twenty-eight hours. The next twenty years would see the zenith of the coaching era in all its glory, with York as one of England's major coaching cities.

Waiting at the *Tavern*
1839

It was about 7 o'clock on a Monday evening in January and a lady and her maid were waiting in the *York Tavern* to meet a passenger on the Leeds coach. On its arrival she went out and paid the coachman, then put her purse back into her reticule which hung on her arm. She had noticed two well-dressed young men hovering near them and her maid saw one of the men stoop down and reach out his arm. The lady felt a pull at the string of her bag, which she quickly placed under her muff. On her return home she found the bottom of her reticule had been cut, as well as her sleeve in two places, but her purse was safe. The women were able to give a good description of the two men to the police and it was hoped there was a good chance of them being found. It was reported that during the previous Sunday evening service in the Minster three ladies had their pockets picked, and there had been a similar incident in Lendal chapel.[3]

The *York Tavern* was one of the city's three main coaching inns, the others being *The George* and the *Black Swan* in Coney Street. All three have long since closed, but at the old entrance to *The George* the wheel marks can still be seen of coaches making the sharp turn from the narrow street into the coachyard.

A timetable of arrivals and departures at the *Black Swan* in 1823 shows just how busy these inns were:

Morning

5.45	Dep.	*The Wellington* to Liverpool
5.45	Dep.	*The Union* to Kendal
7.30	Arr.	*The New Mail* from Liverpool
9.00	Dep.	*The Express* to London
9.00	Dep.	*The Express* to Sheffield and Birmingham
10.00	Dep.	*The Rockingham* to Hull

She noticed two well-dressed men

The London Mail

10.00	Arr.	*The Trafalgar* from Hull
11.00	Arr.	*The True Blue* from Leeds
11.30	Arr.	*The Express* from London
11.30	Arr.	*The Express* from Birmingham and Sheffield
Noon	Arr.	*The Union* from Sheffield
Noon	Dep.	*The Old True Blue* to Scarborough – except Sundays

Afternoon

12.15	Dep.	*The Tally Ho* to Harrogate – Tuesday, Thursday, Saturday
12.30	Arr.	*The True Blue* from Scarborough
1.30	Dep.	*The Union* to Sheffield – except Sundays
1.45	Dep.	*The True Blue* to Leeds
2.00	Dep.	*The Trafalgar* to Hull
2.00	Dep.	*The Express* to Carlisle – Monday, Wednesday, Friday
4.00	Arr.	*The Rockingham* from Hull
7.00	Arr.	*The Union* from Kendal
7.00	Arr.	*The Wellington* from Leeds
7.15	Arr.	*The Mails* from Scarborough and Whitby
8.00	Arr.	*The Mail* from London
8.00	Arr.	*The Wellington* from London
8.00	Arr.	*The Tally Ho* from Harrogate
9.00	Arr.	*The Highflyer* from Edinburgh
10.00	Arr.	*The Express* from Carlisle
11.30	Arr.	*The Mail* from Edinburgh

In all, we have in the region of sixty coaches a day speeding over Ouse Bridge and through the city centre. Others travelled to West Yorkshire and Liverpool from the *Elephant & Castle* in Skeldergate, to Ripon from the *Pack Horse* at the bottom of Micklegate, to Selby from the *Robin Hood* in Castlegate, and to Hull from the *Red Lion* at Monk Bar.

In the narrow medieval streets built for pedestrians and slow moving carts, it was little wonder that there were many accidents.

An old man on an ass
1824

At about 9 o'clock on a Sunday morning in October an old man named Spence was riding his ass along Coney Street. The London Express coach, setting off from the *Black Swan*, came speeding round the corner and the coach guard blew his horn warning of his right of way. Mr Spence tried to move aside but his ass suddenly became stupid and walked straight into the horses. The old man was thrown to the ground and run over by the wheels. He was taken to the county hospital where, the press reported, he lay in a deplorable state.[4]

Riding his ass along Coney Street

Furious driving
1825

On a Tuesday morning in January the following year, a young man was crossing the street at almost the same spot and was knocked down by the vehicle being used to carry mail bags from the *Black Swan* to the post office. He was seriously injured and had to be carried home. The local press was already campaigning against dangerous driving. 'We hope that this, which is not the first accident that has occurred from the above unnecessary and dangerous practice, will prove a sufficient reason for discontinuance.'[5]

A major stopping place in the Great Coaching Era

Snatched from danger
1827

On a Saturday in May there were two coach accidents in virtually the same spot. At 5 o'clock in the afternoon, two army officers were riding in a gig towards the *York Tavern* as the *London Highflyer* was leaving. The two vehicles collided and the gig horses reared, throwing one of the occupants out. He received some injuries and one of the horses was badly cut.

At about 8 o'clock that evening one of the 'Mails' was running at its usual speed in St Helen's Square when a little child ran in front of the horses. The horses all passed over the child without touching it and the driver managed to stop the coach at the very moment when the next move of the wheel would in all probability have crushed it to death. The child was snatched up by a passer-by and escaped serious injury.

A few months later, on the Thursday before Christmas at about 7.30 in the evening, the *Hull Mail* had almost reached the *York Tavern* when it overturned in Coney Street. Workmen had been digging a drain in New Street and had left a heap of earth and stone at the end of the street without any warning lights. One of the passengers was seriously injured and the guard was thrown against the window of Mr Benson's glass shop. Fortunately for him the shutters had been closed.[6]

A press campaign
1829

By 1829, coaching accidents were a frequent occurrence in the city streets and the local press was becoming more critical of coach drivers. On a Sunday evening in April the Edinburgh coach was leaving the city, turning from Little Blake Street (now the much wider Duncombe Place) into Petergate and towards Bootham Bar, when the lead horses turned short and both fell. The press commented 'It is a fortunate circumstance that the coach itself was not overturned of which to the spectators there seemed great danger'.

At about 11 o'clock on an August Monday morning the *Ebor* coach from Leeds to Scarborough had entered the city through Micklegate Bar and was speeding down the hill. Someone noticed that one of the front wheels was almost off and called out a warning but his cries could not be heard above the noise of the coach. The wheel came off opposite North Street and the front of the coach dropped and dragged on the ground until opposite Mr Taylor's tobacconist's shop it fell onto its side with a tremendous crack. Passers-by thought at first that several of the passengers must have been killed. The two gentlemen travelling inside the coach were only slightly injured, but twelve passengers had been travelling on top, where fares were half-price, six men, five women, and a young boy. Some were hurt but it was mostly bruising and there were no bones broken. Fortunately Mr Coates, the

Speeding down the hill from Micklegate Bar

surgeon, was passing by and was able to attend to the injured. Mr Stead of Ripponden, who was on his way to Scarborough to join his family there, suffered a dislocated shoulder and severe cuts to his face and was taken to Mr Rook's *Bridge Hotel*. Mr Woodhead of Leeds was also severely injured and was taken to Mr Taylor's. It was later found that one of the rear wheels had also been loose and that the lynch pins had been removed. This might have happened when the coach was being greased, but there were suspicions that it had been a deliberate act by some wicked and mischievous person on the road.

It was the mail coaches, with tight schedules to keep, that were among the worst offenders. On Wednesday evening of the following week a man was knocked down by one of the mail coaches near Bootham Bar and seriously injured. The press reported 'We cannot but severely condemn the speed at which coaches are daily driven through the streets. It is surprising that more accidents do not happen'.

Stonemason James Sollitt took up the case by applying for a summons against Thomas Wray, driver of the *Edinburgh Mail*. He had been taking a cart full of stone through Bootham Bar when the

Mail crashed into him. His cart was overturned, he was thrown out and suffered a severe gash to the head. He said he had been driving on the left of the road close to the flagstones and that the coach had approached him at a rapid pace but the guard, James Lawrence, told the court that the coach was being driven at no more than the usual speed of nine miles an hour. It was reported that no coachman from the city had a better character for steadiness and sobriety and had been in his present occupation for twenty-six years and was never before complained of. The court imposed a lenient penalty of 20*s*.

One Wednesday the following November the Scarborough coach crashed into a cart which was standing near the *Garrick's Head* in a narrow part of Petergate. The coach broke a window opposite and some of the horses were injured. The press commented 'We should be glad if the commissioners had sufficient funds at command to widen that and other narrow streets in the city'.[7]

A coach out of control
1835

On Boxing Day morning, a Saturday, the *Trafalgar* coach from Hull was approaching the narrow part of Coney Street travelling towards the *York Tavern* when the coachman saw a cart coming in the opposite direction. He called to the cart driver to move over, but the driver refused, and there was a collision. The splinter bar of the coach broke off and became entangled with the horses. The coach was licensed to carry eighteen passengers, but it was not reported how many were on board as they watched the horses stampede down the street with onlookers too terrified to try to stop them. As they reached the *Black Swan* Mr Beaumont, one of the waiters, risked life and limb by springing forward and catching hold of the reins and managed to stop the horses.

On this occasion the press placed the blame firmly on the carter. It reported that the coachman was a very steady man and had driven the night mail for many years.

Some weeks later, on a Sunday evening, the Hull coach met with another accident in the city, overturning when a lynch pin fell out of the axle tree. The thirteen passengers were shocked but sustained no material injuries.[8]

The soot bag
1838

In the dark early hours of a February Friday morning, some merry-makers were returning from the Tradesman's Ball when they saw a bag of soot left by a chimney sweep near the *York Tavern*. Standing opposite was the *Hull Mail*. They opened up the coach and placed the bag on one of the seats. With soot all over their dress vests the culprits were soon apprehended and taken into the coach office where they were booked for damage done to the lining of Her Majesty's coach by their unauthorised passenger.[9]

The press campaign continues
1838

Accidents continued through the summer of 1838 with two in Spurriergate during July. The second, between two Leeds stage coaches, prompted the press to exclaim 'Surely while we have a place in the very centre of the city, in the most frequented and crowded part of which life and limb are every day placed in jeopardy, the city commissioners should seriously give their attention to it'.

Five days later a collision between a cab and the London *Highflyer* resulted in the breakage of watchmaker Mr Howden's shop window and several of his watch glasses. Within a fortnight the *Highflyer* had collided again, this time with two brick carts. 'How long is this state of things to continue?' asked the press.[10]

A drunken coach guard
1839

On a Tuesday evening in July sometime between 8 and 9 o'clock, a former coach guard named Houseman climbed up onto the *Victoria* coach to hitch a ride. He had been drinking and as the coach passed

He fell head-first off his seat

through the streets bystanders noticed that he was very unsteady on his seat. As the coach turned sharply out of Spurriergate towards Ouse Bridge in front of Mr Bewley's tobacconist's, he fell head-first off his seat and the coach ran over his body and one of his arms. He was rushed to surgeon Brown in Castlegate with some very severe injuries, and later taken home.[11]

Seven weeks earlier York's first railway passenger train had left from a temporary terminus outside the city walls, near the western entrance to the present-day station, to join the Leeds–Selby line at Gascoigne Junction. Within ten years it was possible to travel by rail from York to London, and the great British coaching era was almost at an end.

The collapse of Lendal Bridge
1861

Before the 1860s there was only one bridge in York over the River Ouse. At the western edge of the city, near Lendal Tower, a ferryman took passengers across the river for a fee of one halfpenny. The railway station was close to the Lendal crossing and in 1857 it was decided that a girder bridge should replace the ferry.

On 27 September 1861, during the bridge-building, the girders collapsed sending seven workers to their deaths. Early reports said that two were dead and several more missing. The first body to be recovered from the river, found near the sunken girder, was that of

Two were dead and five missing

Luke Brown. The following day the *York Herald* described Luke's body as the most ghastly spectacle and said that his head had been mangled to such a fearful degree as to present the appearance of a hideous mass of pulpy matter. The body was covered and taken to *The Cannon*, an inn built into the city walls on the Minster side of the river and frequented by Sunday afternoon walkers.

For their Sunday entertainment that weekend, crowds gathered at the riverside to see more bodies brought up. Among the bodies were those of twenty-year-old Henry Smith and young Thomas Hoyle, both of nearby Queen Street. Thomas's body was taken to the *Bricklayers Arms* in Tanner's Moat where his sister came along to identify him. She confirmed that he had been working on the bridge and said that he was nine or ten years old.

Lendal Bridge was finally completed and opened in November 1863 to a new design, greatly relieving the congestion on Ouse Bridge. The old girders were sent to Scarborough to be used in the Forge Valley Bridge, and *The Cannon* public house was pulled down.[12]

The wood cart
1877

After the end of the coaching era, private carriages, cab drivers and goods traffic all continued to make the streets a dangerous place for the unsuspecting pedestrian. In April 1832 it had been reported that a horse, harnessed to a cart in Walmgate, took fright and set off at a furious rate. It crashed into the window of the *Lord Nelson* destroying a number of glasses inside the pub.[13]

An incident outside an inn in Coppergate in 1877 had more serious consequences. Little Francis Day Robinson was almost four. His mother had sent his two sisters, aged six and eight, on an errand, but told them not to take him with them because the city streets were so crowded. They took no notice.

Mr Casson of Coppergate looked out of the window of *The Yorkshireman Inn* and saw a large cart loaded with wood and drawn by three horses coming along very slowly from Castlegate. It was being driven on the wrong side of the road to get round a sharp corner without mounting the paving flags. Behind the cart the three children were following, Francis holding onto the wood. Mr Casson's companion cried 'The child will be run over'. He ran outside, followed by Mr Casson, but they were too late to prevent the child from falling beneath the wheels. The driver James Booth still could not see what had happened and they called out to him to stop, but he was unable to pull up for about 20 yards because the hill was so steep and his load weighed about 3 tons. Mr Casson picked the child up and gave him to

Mr Cherry a joiner, who hurried to the house of Mr Hood, the surgeon. The surgeon looked at the child and said he thought he was already dead. Refusing to give up hope they sent for a cab to take Mr Casson and the child to the hospital. The cab had travelled only one street away, to Pavement, when the horse fell and almost threw the passengers out of the vehicle. Mr Casson took another look at the child and now realised there was little to be done but to take the body to the police station.

At the inquest, held at the *Talbot* in Church Street, the coroner's jury gave a verdict of accidental death but added that something should be done to widen Coppergate because of the increase in traffic.[14]

CHAPTER 13

The Game of Chance

A fatal card game at the *Bay Horse*
1839

It was about 4 o'clock on a Tuesday afternoon in April. Shoemaker Edward Hughes was walking past the *Bay Horse* in High Petergate, kept by Thomas and Mary Threpland. Hearing cries of 'Murder!' from inside, he went in and saw several men fighting in the kitchen. A young Irishman was on the floor with a young Englishman on top of him, others were joining in, and a table was thrown into the mêlée. The Irishman was complaining about unfair play and the Englishman said he would serve the Irishman as 'Deaf Burke did Bendigo'. (These two pugilists had fought earlier that year for the championship of England when Burke, the reigning champion, had lost his title and the £220 purse to Bendigo after being disqualified for head-butting.) Seconds were appointed for each man and both stripped to the waist. After fighting for some minutes the Englishman followed the example of his hero by striking his opponent with a foul blow. The low punch

A young Irishman was on the floor

caused the young Irishman to fall to the floor through his second's arms. A surgeon, Mr Husband, was sent for and pronounced the young man dead.

The Englishman, using language as foul as his tactics, swore he could kill a dozen such Irishmen. The body was carried outside and laid on the flagstones, where a shocked crowd gathered. The other fighter, later identified as Thomas Fawcett, emerged from the inn and was pursued by the crowd in the direction of the Shambles but made his escape. During the evening a large crowd gathered outside the *Bay Horse* for news, and at first it was reported that the incident had taken place in the street.

The inquest was held at 2 o'clock the following afternoon at the *White Swan* in Goodramgate. The murdered man had been identified as Thomas Moran, a labourer who had lived in the Water Lanes, and it was said that he was normally a quiet man but rather quarrelsome when in liquor. It seemed that both men had been willing to fight, but a warrant was issued for Fawcett's arrest.

On the Thursday afternoon Thomas Moran was buried in St Mary's churchyard in Castlegate. It was reported that there was a mourning coach but the crowd had not been numerous.

In July the two men who acted as seconds, William Harton and John Cobb, were tried for manslaughter but found not guilty. Fawcett had still not been caught.[1]

'The devil made me do it'
1824

On Tuesday night, 26 May, a Sheffield wine merchant by the name of Pearson was staying at the *White Horse* in Skeldergate. Also staying there was a respectable-looking man named John Wilkinson, putting up for the races. On the Wednesday morning, as Mr Pearson came downstairs, Wilkinson entered the wine merchant's bedroom and stole some banknotes to the value of £30 upwards, six silk hand-kerchiefs, a shirt, and some other items. The alarm was raised. The thief was followed and arrested when he offered the Bank of England £30 note as payment for some goods. He said to the magistrates in true Scottish dialect 'I am guilty sure enough. It was the devil, nothing but the devil, that made me do it'.[2]

Mysterious poisoning of a Whitby seaman
1885

William Knaggs from Ruswarp, near Whitby, had been a chief mate in the merchant navy but he had not worked for the past eighteen months. He now spent most of his time drinking and attending race meetings and often complained to his housemate Thomas Macintosh about his losses, but he never said how much. On Wednesday 26 August he was in York for the races and at about 11 o'clock in the morning he called at the *Black Swan* to book his room. There he met Alfred Robinson, the boots, whom he had known for about six months, and they had a long debate about which horse would win the Ebor Handicap later that day.

He returned at about 7 o'clock that evening and, although he often arrived having had a few to drink, on that particular evening he was reasonably sober having nothing more to spend. He told Alfred 'I've lost £120 today'. About half an hour later Alfred heard the bell in William's room ring very loudly but when he went upstairs he found the door locked. William called to him 'Come in, I'm bad' and Alfred broke the door open to find William standing at the end of the bed. The seaman told Alfred he had taken poison instead of brandy and he would be dead within an hour. Dr Rose was called immediately.

Meanwhile chambermaid Fanny Hickling, heard that William had taken the poison by mistake and gave him some mustard and water, but it did not help. Seeing them searching for the bottle which might have contained the poison William said 'Look in the fireplace', and they found a bottle there which had been bought in Whitby. It was marked 'Laudanum – poison'.

The doctor soon arrived but found William in bed in a semi-conscious state and the seaman soon became quite comatose. The doctor stayed with him about six hours until he died at about 2 o'clock in the morning. The inquest was held in the *Black Swan* that evening, when a verdict was given of 'suicide whilst of sound mind'.[3]

The hanging of Snowy Marsh
1880

It was about 7 o'clock on a May Thursday morning at George Dyson's *Railway Hotel* in Tanner Row. A servant climbed up into the hayloft behind the hotel and stepped back in horror. In the grey morning light he saw a man hanging from a beam. The servant edged closer and saw the rope round the man's neck – the blackened face and protruding tongue were a sure sign that he was quite dead. The body was quickly cut down and the police were informed.

The man had been seen in the hotel yard the previous day but had not been staying there. In the hope that he might be identified, the local press printed a description of him. He was said to be about forty years of age, five feet eight inches in height with brown hair, grey eyes and clean shaven. They said that he had been dressed in a black worsted coat, a vest, grey trousers, laced boots, a black silk hat, silver

A man, hanging in the grey morning light

plaid tie, checked cotton shirt with grey undershirt, drawers and socks all in good condition.

It was suspected that the man was William Marsh, known in racing circles as Snowy, a well-known racing tout. The inquest, in the hotel, was adjourned until there was positive identification, and this was given by his brother-in-law, a Mr Pinder from Doncaster.

When the inquest was resumed the coroner was told that the body was found with very little money. It was supposed that Snowy had lost heavily at the races that day and returning to the *Railway Hotel* in a state of dejection had taken his own life. The possibility of robbery and murder did not seem to have occurred to anyone and a verdict of suicide was given.[4]

CHAPTER 14

Season's Greetings

An Irish Christmas
1830

It was Christmas Day at the *White Swan* in Pavement. In the taproom there were about fourteen Irishmen who, the magistrates were later told, 'had partaken rather too freely of the juice of Sir John Barleycorn'. A number of Englishmen were also in the room 'quietly drinking', it was said, when an Irishmen struck one of them on the head with a poker. The Irish party then began to smash the tables and in the general free-for-all a number of other customers were seriously injured. The patrol arrived in force and managed to arrest six of the Irishmen, John, Peter, James and George Rigan, Peter Smith and a man named Connor. The rest escaped.

They began to smash the tables

The unfortunate six appeared at the Guildhall in the New Year and George Rigan stated their case. 'We came to York, your worship, on Christmas day to enjoy ourselves and drink a glass of liquor, your honour, being old customers and had six or eight half pints of rum which made us rather groggy, your worship. These bloody Englishmen, seeing what state we were in, began calling us after our own dear country 'Pats', your honour and, if it please your worship, Peter Rigan thinking this not quite right let slip at the English and this began the row.' Peter Rigan denied having used violence. 'I never struck any of them', he said. Peter Smith, described by the reporter as 'a quaint-looking Irish character', said 'Oh by St Patrick your honour, don't it look as if they've been fighting among themselves and not with ourselves, for, by my faith, they're all back and blue and ourselves as clane and nate as new-peeled shillelaghs'. They were each fined £2 and, being unable to pay, were sent to the House of Correction.[1]

A ten-stone Christmas pie
1829

Thomas Sanderson, landlord of the *City Arms* in the cattle market, had a Christmas treat for his numerous friends. He served up a pie weighing ten stones baked by Mr Cox near Micklegate Bar. The contents included two geese, a hare, two ox tongues, a brace of pheasants, three braces of partridges, a brace of woodcocks, a couple of wild ducks and guinea fowl, four rabbits, a stone of pork and a stone of mutton. The press reported that more substantial fare was seldom met with nor had it ever been served out with greater hospitality.[2]

The contents included two geese

Compliments of the season
1873

At 11.15 on Christmas night landlord William Heslop of the *Old George* in Fossgate was standing at his door. As PC Tattersfield was walking past the landlord wished him the compliments of the season and invited him in for a drink of rum and water as a Christmas box. The policeman gladly accepted but on going back out into the cold night he was met by police Inspector Monkman. He was accused by the inspector of being drunk and was sent home. On New Year's Day William had to appear at the Guildhall, charged with supplying liquor to a policeman while on duty. He admitted the charge but said it was only a matter of kindness and he had not intended to break the licensing laws. The magistrates at first decided to find him guilty with a small 1*s* fine. On being reminded that the minimum fine was 20*s* they changed their verdict and dismissed the case.[3]

A Christmas raffle
1880

Shortly before Christmas, landlord Richard Cowper was holding a Saturday evening raffle for a goose in the *Pack Horse* at the bottom of Micklegate. He collected 6*d* from each of his customers and then asked them each to roll the set of dice. One of his customers was not happy. Mark Wrightson, a farmer from Rufforth, claimed he had paid and refused to shake the dice when he was asked for his money. He went to the police and reported that the landlord was allowing gaming on his premises.

In court it was said in defence that holding raffles before Christmas was common practice in the city's pubs and although strictly speaking it was wrong, it was no different from raffles held at Christmas bazaars. The magistrates believed that Mr Cowper had broken the law and that they had no alternative to but to convict him, but they fined him the smallest amount they could, 2*s* 6*d* without costs.[4]

Gradually the police managed to prevent the raffling of geese and other Christmas fare in the city's inns and by the end of the century such raffles were being officially run from tobacconists' shops.

A New Year's dinner at the *George*
1801

On a Thursday morning, the first day of 1801 was celebrated in York by the ringing of bells to celebrate the union between the kingdoms of Ireland and Great Britain. In Blake Street, the York Volunteers assembled to fire three volleys. The 18th hussar dragoons, in their

blue tunics and brown fur hats, marched into town from the new
Fulford barracks, through the streets, and fired a *fou-de-joie*.

That evening, the hussar officers attended a dinner at the *George
Hotel* in Coney Street. It was late when they left and rather than
return quietly to their barracks they pervaded the streets with their
band of music. The press commented 'It is with no small regret we
have to announce that much disturbance and annoyance took place in
consequence, many of the peaceable inhabitants on their return to
their homes being insulted and several of them wounded with the
swords of the officers'.[5]

They pervaded the streets with their band of music

CHAPTER 15

Soldier, Soldier

Billeting in the city

The billeting of soldiers in the city had long been a bone of contention with the landlords and towards the end of the eighteenth century it had been common practice for between two hundred and a thousand troops to be billeted in the city inns, up to 30 per cent of the adult male population. With only forty of the York's 180 inns having stabling accommodation the cavalry horses had taken up almost 10 per cent of the inns' stabling capacity and in the 1790s, after many complaints from the city's innkeepers, a permanent cavalry barracks was built in Fulford, stabling over 250 horses. In 1861 the barracks was enlarged to accommodate 1,000 men and 600 horses.

However, the infantry barracks, which eventually housed 1,100 men, were not built until 1877–80 and for most of the nineteenth century innkeepers still had to suffer billeting of foot soldiers. Their only consolation was that most of the soldiers' disposable income found its way into their tills. In April 1816, the innkeepers met at the

The soldiers' income found its way into their tills

Robin Hood to petition the Government over the additional duties on licences and billeting of soldiers.[1]

Fines for turning recruits away

In 1843 landlord George Baines of the *Durham Ox* in North Street was charged with having on 3 January refused to entertain and provide for William Cockerill and John Saddler, two privates in the Buckinghamshire Regiment of Foot. He told the court that he had one soldier billeted at the time and the two men came at a time when the beds were engaged by members of his family. He had thought the men were sent to him by mistake. The court fined him £2.[2]

In May 1854 Francis Redfern of the *Elephant & Castle* in Skeldergate faced a similar charge. On a Saturday evening a sergeant took a recruit along after 9 o'clock to ask for billeting or to be paid out. Mr Redfern said that accommodation was offered but the recruit refused and asked for money. It was said that the soldier had now gone to London and the Lord Mayor dismissed the charge.[3]

Four years later John Dawson, landlord of the *Drover's Arms*, and his wife must have thought they also had a good case for not housing two recruits. Mrs Dawson appeared in court to answer the charge, stating her husband was not at home on the day the recruits had called. She said she had gone to bed shortly before 10 o'clock and had not heard them call. She was also fined £2.[4]

'Damn soldiers, and the Queen too!'
1845

On a Saturday morning towards the end of January, two privates of the South Lincolnshire regiment came into *The Ship* in Skeldergate and asked for hot dinners. The landlord, Nicholas Austick, came in and saw them and said 'Damn soldiers, and the Queen too!' The men's sergeant remonstrated with him for his discourteous conduct and disrespect for the Queen and the case came to court. The landlord accused the soldiers of foul language but the case was proven against him, mainly because of his comments about the Queen. He was given a mitigated fine of 40*s*.[5]

Sleeping in the stable
1850

On a Tuesday afternoon in April a private of the 41st regiment was billeted at the *City Arms* in the Cattle Market. He complained to the Lord Mayor that his sleeping accommodation was outside the house over a detached stable and 'in a very unwholesome state and not fit to put your lordship's dog in, much less a Christian'. Thomas Stephenson, the landlord, claimed it was purpose-built by the council, and that it had been occupied by his own servants as well as soldiers, and was as comfortable as anyone could wish. The ostler supported this and said the room was not over a stable but a lumber room. The case was adjourned for an inspection of the premises to be made, and the parties did not reappear, apparently having come to an agreement.[6]

Destroying the house
1855

Robert Cameron, a recruit, was billeted at the *White Horse* in Skelder-gate. On Friday 5 January the landlord, Joseph Cowper, deciding the recruit had had too much to drink, asked him to get to bed. Cameron became violent and broke a window pane valued at 3*s* 6*d*. At the Guildhall the following day he was ordered to pay for the damage or go to prison for seven days. Mr Cowper told the court that he thought it was very hard that he should have to accommodate recruits and have his house destroyed into the bargain.[7]

A disturbance at dinner
1858

Two days after Christmas, George Wright, a private of the 75th Highland Regiment, was eating his dinner in the kitchen of *The Crown* in Parliament Street, when he heard the landlady cry out in the main room of the inn. He rushed through to the room to find Sergeant

Trying to protect the landlady

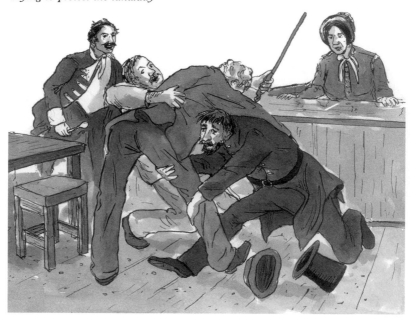

Blaney trying to protect the landlady and her customers from a man armed with a poker. He tried to help the sergeant, who was being hit and kicked in the face, but was struck by the assailant across the hands and arms, and PC Worcester who was called to the inn was also assaulted.

Anthony David Dowd was charged the following day at the Guildhall, with having been drunk and disorderly and assault, but the sergeant was in bed owing to the injuries he had received and the case was adjourned. At the later hearing the sergeant gave evidence. Dowd was fined 40s and costs for the assault on the sergeant, and 20s plus costs for the assault on the policeman. In the event of non-payment he was to receive a sentence of a month and two weeks' imprisonment.[8]

A new suit of clothes
1831

In April, a young soldier named Bew, serving in the Prince of Wales' Dragoon Guards, went into Mr Burr's saddler's shop in Coney Street and asked to cash a cheque for £30. He said that the banks were closed, and that his commanding officer who was staying at the nearby *Black Swan* needed the money urgently. To convince the saddler, the dragoon took him into the inn, taking care to avoid any of the staff, and showed him a room which he said was his master's. Mr Burr was convinced and handed over the money.

The young soldier immediately went off to buy himself a suit of clothes with the money, and pleased with his success, he continued to use the same trick on other traders until their suspicions were aroused.

One followed him but, instead of returning to the *Black Swan*, Bew went into a house in one of the Water Lanes with which we are already well-acquainted. Police searched the house and in an upstairs recess they noticed his leg sticking out from his hiding place. He was arrested, wearing his new suit, and it was said that he had also treated his ill-reputed lady companion to a new gown and other clothing. He appeared at the Guildhall, charged with obtaining money under false pretences.[9]

A cavalryman at the *Full Moon*
1866

Private James Cowan of the King's Royal Irish Regiment of Light Dragoons was on leave and staying at the *Full Moon* in Walmgate. On a Saturday morning in January the cavalryman, believing that some of his property had been stolen, decided to pack his kit bag and move to another inn. Landlord John Halloran, asked him to let him see inside the kit bag but Cowan refused and the landlord threw him down and beat him, breaking one of his teeth.

In court the next Thursday, the landlord's son admitted that his father had struck the first blow. In defence, Mr Halloran said that some clothing was missing from the inn and he had suspected Cowan of theft. The magistrates found in the soldier's favour and fined the landlord half a crown.[10]

A ragamuffin recruit
1858

On 18 March two recruits presented themselves at the *Square & Compass* in Garden Place and landlord Thomas Garnett agreed that they could be billeted there. At about 6 o'clock on the evening one of the recruits, named Valentine, returned to the inn with a mutton chop and asked for it to be cooked. Mrs Garnett said he could not sit in the inn and he must leave the house until bedtime, 'for tradesmen and others who come here with gold pins and studs will not sit with such a ragamuffin as you'. He left and found lodgings elsewhere and in the morning he reported the incident to Sergeant Atkinson who went along to the inn. Mrs Garnett told the sergeant 'I will not have the recruit, neither for good nor bad'.

When the landlord was summoned to the Guildhall the following week, he complained of the sergeant's insulting behaviour towards his wife and of the 'dodges' practised by recruits in order to get money by the paying-out system. A witness was called to say that the sergeant, on leaving, said to Mrs Garnett 'I'll make you whistle for it', but he denied having said it. The Lord Mayor said that publicans were not only obliged to find lodgings for those billeted upon them, but also accommodation and shelter for them by day. He thought that the landlord had been under a misapprehension of the law and fined him the minimum amount of 40*s*.[11]

Enlisting at the *Hand & Heart*
1852

The *Hand & Heart* in St Sampson's Square was one of the city's bases for recruitment. On New Year's Day Corporal Daniel Bond of the 2nd Somersetshire Regiment was there and enlisted a man calling himself William Turner into the St Helena regiment. The new recruit then went into hiding but was found a few days later and arrested as a deserter. Under his real name of Patrick Dolin he was sent to the House of Correction to be dealt with 'as the Secretary of War might think proper'.

The inn continued as a recruitment centre for some years and in November 1860 when the till in the kitchen was broken into and £2 in silver was stolen it was suspected that one of the soldiers sleeping there was responsible.[12]

'You'll never make a soldier'
1858

John James had been a corporal in the Royal Irish Dragoon Guards and now, in his new vocation as landlord of the *Duke of York* in Walmgate, he recruited soldiers at his inn. On Saturday 4 February he invited John Molland of Brawby near Malton to enlist. Molland swore that he had never enlisted before or belonged to the militia and accepted the Queen's shilling. The landlord kept him at the inn until

Sunday morning, when the medical inspector recognised him as being enlisted before and being rejected as unfit for service. The next day Molland appeared in court but was acquitted on a legal technicality. The Lord Mayor advised him to return to the place to which he belonged as it was evident that he would 'never make a soldier'.[13]

Arresting a deserter, 1858

The following month it was reported that a deserter had been arrested by landlord William Harrison at *The Eagle* in Goodramgate. The inn was a meeting house for the military and he recognised Francis Feely who had been reported as a deserter from the North Riding Regiment of Foot, and delivered him into custody. Feely admitted that he was a recruit but complained that the landlord had detained him only for the reward of a sovereign.[14]

A soldier turned beggar
1869

John Wood, a discharged soldier, now made his living by begging and was hardly able to walk. Between 9 and 10 o'clock on Thursday evening 28 January he went into the *Old Turk's Head* at the top of the Shambles and asked Robert Dutton the landlord for a penny or two. The landlord refused and Wood responded by breaking two squares of glass in the window. He was tried the following day and in spite of his infirmity he was sent to the House of Correction for fourteen days.[15]

An army pensioner
1848

Nathaniel Firth had once been a private in the 76th Regiment of Foot, which had been known in Napoleonic times as 'the Hindoostan Regiment'. Now, aged about sixty-five, he was an army pensioner. On the first Wednesday in January he went into the *Old Malt Shovel* in Walmgate where the army pensions were paid but when he arrived he complained of feeling ill. He called for a glass of brandy and water, which the landlord Mr Broadmead brought to him, but before he could put the glass to his mouth he fell down suddenly upon the floor in a fit of apoplexy. He was carried into the back kitchen and Mr Mann the surgeon was sent for immediately. At first it was thought he would quickly recover but, although the surgeon bled him and tried other ways to resuscitate him, he died within a few minutes. The inquest was held in the same inn, and the usual verdict of 'died by the visitation of God' was given.[16]

CHAPTER 16

Trouble on the Streets

Tommy knockers
1810

On Saturday evening last a little after 10 o'clock three persons who had the appearance of military gentlemen shamelessly amused themselves by alarming the families of Castlegate Lane and all along Castlegate by violent and continued knocking at almost every door.

We wish they had been better employed. They disgrace the military character by such foolish and rude conduct. They should recollect that they are appointed for the protection of our country, not for the annoyance of its wives and children.[1]

Forty years later little had changed. It was reported that on Sunday 22 December 1850 at 4 o'clock in the morning a party of young men in Castlegate were ringing bells and rapping at doors. The police took one of them, Edward Hunter, into custody but the following day the magistrates released him after a caution and payment of costs.[2]

A riot at the *Spotted Dog*
1832

Late on New Year's Eve a young tailor boy, Leonard Brown, was on his way back to work in Fossgate after dinner. To get there from his home in Peaseholme Green he had to walk through St Saviourgate. Outside the *Spotted Dog* he saw that a massive crowd had gathered. Press reports described several hundred people behaving disgracefully, shouting and fighting in the street. Leonard stopped to watch the fun as John Milner took an axe and began to smash the front door down. There were also a large number of people inside the house, throwing missiles at the crowd, and after about five minutes Leonard was hit over the head with half a brick thrown from a window. He was covered in blood and would have fallen under the feet of the rioting crowd, but the wall he was leaning against kept him upright and he was helped to safety.

Leonard appeared as a witness in the Guildhall on 4 January with a large plaster on his head, when John Milner and his wife Dinah were charged with forcibly taking possession of the inn. The brewer John

Kilby offered bail for them. Another eight men were in the dock charged with affray and were fined considerable sums ranging from £25 to £100.

There was a further hearing scheduled for 12 April at the Guildhall, when Leonard was due to present himself as a key witness, but the court was informed he was unable to attend because of a headache from his wound. The hearing was postponed until the following day when it transpired that Leonard had met George Holmes, one of the prisoners, in the street the previous day. The prisoner persuaded Leonard to go with him to the Turf Coffee House near St Sampson's Square where he bought the boy a pint of ale and a glass of rum. Soon they were joined by the other prisoners, who took turns to buy him ale and rum until he was drunk.

This time nine men appeared in court. They were all from Acomb, and although a witness was produced to the good character of one of them it was found that he and another had already served a six-month prison sentence. Many inhabitants of Acomb had signed a petition against the men, appealing that their lives and property were in danger from them. Found guilty of riot and endangering life and property, most were given three months' hard labour, but a twelve-month sentence was given to the two who had already served time.[3]

A fight with the landlady
1868

At about 8 o'clock on a Sunday evening in February, PC Markham was called to Carmelite Street, named after the friary that once stood

Challenging the landlady to a fight

close by. Since its demolition at the time of the reformation it seems that the street's reputation had also disintegrated, and the policeman found a crowd of a hundred people gathered outside a beer house there. In their midst was Catherine McGrail of nearby Garden Place, challenging the landlady to a fight.

In court the next Thursday she told the magistrates she had been thrown out of the house, but that her husband was still inside drinking and she would not go home without him. She had been before the bench on five previous occasions, and this time the court fined her 5s.[4]

Escape from the *Black Boy*
1840

On the afternoon of Wednesday 22 July, Jane Gowland had been acquitted of the alleged murder in Acomb of her illegitimate child. That evening her husband took her to the *Black Boy* in North Street but they were followed by a large crowd hooting and jeering at them. The landlady, Ann Bowser, was obliged to lock the house for safety, while Mrs Gowland was taken ill with fear. At about 9 o'clock Mrs Bowser managed to disguise Mrs Gowland and get her out through a passage to St John's church next door. It was not until an hour later that the crowd learned of her escape and dispersed.[5]

Rioting in Bedern

Bedern, a small enclave off Goodramgate, had some of the worst accommodation in the city. Anyone walking down this narrow street today might find it hard to imagine that in the first half of the nineteenth century it was home to half a dozen public houses. One of the respectable families living here in 1840 was that of Mr Swales, a schoolmaster. At 2.30 on Sunday morning, 7 June, his wife was woken by the noise from the neighbouring *Slipper* public house. From her bedroom she could see into the window of the pub, where a group of men were fighting, armed with pokers and fire tongs.

Landlord William Smith was accused of allowing drunkenness in his house and the case came to court the next day. Mrs Swales told the Lord Mayor that she had seen one of the accused, Thomas Pullen of Coffee Yard, brandishing a pair of tongs out in the pub yard, and later leave with a woman who, she supposed, was drunk.

George Hall, a paper stainer, took up the story. He lived in Far Water Lane and drinking in the slums of Bedern was for him perhaps home from home. He had been drinking heavily with four of his friends in the *Cross Keys* in Bedern, and at about an hour after midnight they decided to try for a pint or two at the neighbouring *Slipper*. The door was locked but they waited in the passage, sheltering from the pouring rain of a typical British summer. Their opportunity came as the door was opened to allow two customers to leave. They and another group of hopeful late-night drinkers burst in but the landlord said he would not pour another drink that night for anyone living. Mrs Swales witnessed what followed from the safety of her bedroom window, but it transpired that Thomas Pullen had been one of four or five bona fide drinkers still in the *Slipper* and had tried to help the landlord to turn out the offenders. He said he had been there since about 11.30 and at about 1.30 his wife had called to bring him home.

The Lord Mayor said that the case against the landlord had not been clearly proven, but commented that it was not the first time there had been disturbances at the *Slipper*. Magistrate Holtby was less generous with his remarks, saying that it was one of the worst houses in town and warning the landlord to be on his guard in future.[6]

On Thursday 17 April 1851 Ann Turner and Ann Robinson were charged with being common prostitutes and fighting in Bedern, and sent to prison for seven days. Fifteen-year-old Oswald Barker was also charged with assaulting Ann Hunter there at 10.30 on the same evening. He had taken some indecent liberties with her and she slapped his face, whereupon he hit her in the face with a half-brick. The girl Robinson confirmed the evidence and the Lord Mayor said that however disreputable her course of life she had a right to be protected and the youth was sent to the House of Correction for twenty-one days' hard labour.

Five months later improvements to Bedern were proposed. The small area was described as a harbour of vice and infamy. It was said that Bedern has long been known as a sort of Irish Republic where the greatest vagabonds from the Emerald Isle have been accustomed to emigrate to the horror of the entire neighbourhood.[7]

It was the first day of July 1866, shortly before 8 o'clock on a Sunday evening, and Bedern was nearly full of half-frenzied and quarrelsome men, fighting, screaming and hooting. Respectable passers-by in Goodramgate hurried on to avoid the missiles which were being thrown in all directions and the police were called. Incredibly, only one man was sent, officer Robert Dickinson. He found the streets strewn with bricks and rubbish. Windows and a city lamp were smashed, and piles of stones ready for use by the rival antagonists. His authority was challenged and there was little he could do as the riot continued for another two hours.

The riot continued for another 2 hours

Michael Flanagan of Aldwark, the man who had challenged him, appeared in court the following day, along with Anthony Caffrey and John Nelson, who were given twenty-one and fourteen days respectively.[8]

The Troubles in Walmgate

Bedern was rivalled as an outpost of the Emerald Isle only by Walmgate, which filled with immigrants in the 1840s and 1850s. St George's Catholic church was opened here in 1850 to serve the new community, taking as its parish colours the green and red of Mayo, the county from which most of it parishioners originated.

By 1852 Walmgate boasted fifteen public houses and by the end of the century the number had grown to twenty, an average of one every thirty paces. The chronic poverty of the area is reflected in its one in three infant mortality rate in 1888. In the neighbouring streets there were more pubs, one of them being the *Craven Ox Head* in George Street. Built in the 1840s, it later became the *Newcastle Arms*. It was here in April 1851 that the inquest was held on James Finney, an Irish orange seller, who had been killed in Long Close Lane. His daughter Bridget told the jury that she believed, from what he said, that he had been about fifty years of age.

On display in the inquest room were a paving stone, a long sweeping brush handle broken in two, a poker, and a whip-stick with nails and lead attached to one end. All of these were said to have been used in the affray, involving about six men and two or three women, in which James died. Three brothers had been arrested during the fighting and later went to court accused of the killing: Michael, Henry and James Donalin were from county Sligo, a different part of Ireland from James. Eventually two of them were acquitted but Michael, who threw the slab at his victim and beat him with a poker, was found guilty. He was said to have had an otherwise excellent character and was sentenced to only three months' hard labour.[9]

The *Sons of Erin*
1863

In 1863 John McQuade was landlord of the *Sons of Erin* beer house in Walmgate. He appeared in court in April, accused of keeping his house open after hours, his defence being that he did not know what time it was. The hearing was suspended when magistrates heard that police had again visited the *Sons of Erin* after closing time a few nights later and found another fifteen men there drinking beer. The landlord said that they had come in for a glass of beer for their supper after he had closed the house, but could provide no defence when the police found two prostitutes there later that night. At the second hearing he was fined half a crown for each offence.

Within six weeks PC Kinson visited the *Sons of Erin* again and found several hundred people outside. The doors to the house were bolted, and when he eventually gained access he found almost a dozen men and women rolling around in the back room in what he described as an indiscriminate fight. He witnessed a similar scene in the front room and it took him half an hour to quell the disturbance while the landlord nonchalantly looked on. This time Mr McQuade's fine was 20s (£1). It was reported that the usual excessive amount of cross-swearing took place between the defendants in court while the magistrates spent a considerable time trying to decide on which of the sons and daughters of Erin were to blame.[10]

'A Secret Society'

Anthony Battle lived in Long Close Lane, off Walmgate, with his brother John and other members of his family. For more than twenty years they lived at odds with their many of their neighbours, regarded as police informers by the members of the society they refused to join.

At 8 o'clock on a Sunday evening in November 1851, Anthony was in the *Square and Compass*, a few doors from his home. Also present were two Englishmen who lodged there and half a dozen Irishmen. One of the Englishmen handed Anthony a glass of beer in what the Irishmen seem to have believed to have been payment for his services. Two of them jumped across the table, cursing him in Irish, and attacked him. The other four joined in, grabbing fire tongs and a poker and bringing in some paving slabs. Mary Smith, the landlady, called for the police and PC Sweeting forced his way in and eventually restored order. Badly cut around the face, Anthony came to court the following Thursday, where four of his assailants stood accused. Anthony John and Thomas Gallagher and John Naylis all claimed that Anthony had been the aggressor but were each fined 40s (£2) with the threat of a month in the House of Correction if they failed to pay.[11]

Year after year the feud continued and in May 1863 Anthony was attacked in the *Brewers Arms* in Walmgate. He had entered the house at 11 o'clock in the company of two other men and had sat down to drink with them. It was the turn of Michael Brennan of Long Close Lane to be fined, and by this time the penalty had risen to £5. In the likely event of being unable to pay, he faced two months in the House of Correction.[12]

In November of that year there were more disturbances. In one of them, unable to track down Anthony, a group of neighbours cornered his brother John, close to Anthony's home. Having hit him over the head with an iron bar, they bludgeoned him to the ground and kicked him. The first court hearing was postponed because of John's dangerous condition, and some days later Peter Ryan confessed to his part and was given a month's hard labour. Two others, Thomas O'Hara and Francis Scott, received two months for giving false evidence but John Scott, who had struck the first blow, had gone to ground.[13]

That week, Father Holland, parish priest of St George's church, was moved to write an open letter defending the majority of his parishioners and condemning those who resorted to violence.

> There are here around us and in Bedern about a dozen men of bold and cruel stamp who are placed beyond the scope of all moral restraint by having joined a secret society, the name of which is changed occasionally for purposes known to themselves. They know that any deed short of murder is visited by a fine or short imprisonment.
>
> The whole neighbourhood lives in terror of their name and many more are forced into their conspiracies as a safer alternative to taking the law as a guarantee to their independence. By night in a state of partial drunkenness they venture into the streets to challenge or seeking cause of provocation. A great crowd of the curious or well-meaning is immediately created. The disgraceful scene is called an Irish row and hundreds of sober and industrious people suffer in reputation and pocket with the few who are guilty.
>
> This is the history of last week's occurrence but rather more tragical. The victim, a blameless youth, whom they handled barbarously instead of his brother for the disappointment they felt in failing to discover him as he became a marked man by the fact of having a disagreement with this faction
>
> T Holland, St George's presbytery, Walmgate.[14]

It would have come as no consolation to Father Holland that the violence was not all one way, and the following April Anthony was charged with assaulting Michael Brogan in the *Bay Horse* in Walmgate. A surgeon's certificate was produced in court to say that the victim had been severely injured about his head and body and that his life was in danger. A week later he appeared in court and withdrew the charges.[15]

On Sunday evening, 3 November 1867, John Battle was drinking ginger beer in Hannan's Beer House in George Street. His wife came in and signalled to him and he got up to leave. The nine others drinking there had been keeping a close eye on him, and all rushed at him as he stood up. As James Brennan lashed him across the shoulders with a loaded whip, he tried to protect his head, only to be smashed in the face with a stone wielded by Michael Rohan. With a broken nose, two black eyes and numerous other injuries, John had to take a fortnight off work. The two Irish labourers more than made up for this, each being sentenced to a year's hard labour. The magistrate asked John if the attack had any connection to a brotherhood, but John replied that it was too dangerous a question for him to answer. The magistrate then turned to the two assailants and told them that if they came among Englishmen they must behave with the same propriety of conduct as Englishmen were disposed to do, and no exception must be given to Irishmen to commit assaults either on persons belonging to their own nation or any other.[16]

No sooner had John recovered than he was again attacked this time by James Flannagan and others while out drinking with his wife in the *Square and Compass*. When Mrs Battle tried to defend him, James picked up a metal spittoon and hit them both with it. They fled outside, pursued by their attackers and PC Precious told the court that had he not intervened John would barely have escaped with his life.

After the attack, James Flannagan left the city but broke his leg and was arrested and brought before the magistrates. Ann Routledge, his sister, had testified a few days previously in favour of James Brennan and Michael Rohan, and now she came forward in her brother's defence. She said that John had started the violence by challenging any of the others to a fight, and that Mrs Battle had picked up the spittoon and hit James in the face with it. The magistrates doubted her testimony and committed James for trial. For suspected Feinian intimidation he was sentenced to five years' penal servitude.

Meanwhile, the Battle brothers continued to attract trouble and Anthony was still putting in court appearances in 1874.[17]

CHAPTER 17

Demon Drink

Shocking depravity
1855

In 1855 the *Shoulder of Mutton* in Middle Water Lane, which we have
already visited, was kept by Richard Thomas. On a Friday evening in
August a married woman named Ellen MacDonald was drinking
there. She wanted another glass of ale but had spent all of her money,
and she offered to sell her stockings to the landlord for 1½*d*. He
offered her 1*d* and then bought her shoes for another 1*d*, her apron for
2*d*, her stays for 1*d*, and her chemise for 2*d*. Soon she had sold all of
her clothes and a lodger named Smith put her in his waistcoat and
slop shirt. She immediately sold the waistcoat for 1*d* and the shirt for
2*d*. Eventually the landlord told her to go home but she replied 'I
can't go home in this state! Give me something to put on'.

Shortly after midnight she was found by PC Robinson, completely
naked, sitting on a step in Castlegate. He took off his coat to wrap

She offered to sell her stockings to the landlord

round her and arrested her for being drunk and incapable. She was brought to the Guildhall later that day but the case was adjourned for further enquiries to be made. She was later fined 5s and costs, but having no money she was sent to the House of Correction for a week.

The case was raised at the brewster sessions a few days later, when Middle Water Lane was described as being 'frequented by the worst characters, where they arrange their plans for the commission of crime probably in the heat of intoxication'. Magistrate Boltby said that scarcely a responsible person would go along that street, either by day or by night (although we know that a few months earlier the Lord Mayor had admitted to passing by often), and he suggested that the magistrates should adopt some plan to put a stop to the state of things. He drew special attention to the *Shoulder of Mutton* reminding his colleagues that in the case of a beer house, after its third conviction by magistrates, they not only had the power of suppressing the house but of taking care that the landlord should have his licence withdrawn for a lengthened period. Landlord Thomas described Mrs MacDonald as one of the worst characters. He had given her 3d for her lodgings and had been upstairs when someone had put her out. Nevertheless, the magistrates withheld his licence.[1]

Stealing boots at the *Wellington*
1887

At about 3 o'clock on Monday afternoon, 28 March, Elizabeth Pollard, a married woman from Aldwark, went into the *Wellington Inn* in Goodramgate. Although she was the worse for drink, she was served with a glass of beer by the landlord's sixteen-year-old daughter. Elizabeth left the inn but returned at 4 o'clock when the landlord's daughter served her with more beer. Elizabeth also paid for drinks for Henry Carney and John Judge who she met there. Like Elizabeth, they were both drunk and soon afterwards Henry Carney said 'Let's have her boots'. Judge then threw her down and held her while Carney pulled her boots off. They took them to Mr Morrison's shop and pawned them for 3s, which they returned with to buy more drinks for the three of them.

Frederick Hope, the landlord, had not been in the house at the time and when he returned he ordered Mrs Pollard out several times. At 5 o'clock a police sergeant arrived and found a number of people inside who were very drunk, including Mrs Pollard. The landlord's daughter told the sergeant that she had refused to serve Mrs Pollard and had asked her to leave but she had refused to go, complaining that her boots had been stolen. There was also a soldier in the *Wellington*, to whom she had served only two pints of beer and a bottle of ginger ale, who was taken into custody for being drunk and disorderly after leaving.

In court the following day Mrs Pollard admitted that she was drunk at the time and said she did not wish to press charges. The two men pleaded guilty, saying it was 'all a drunken affair', and were each sentenced to seven days with hard labour. The magistrates ordered that the boots be returned to Mrs Pollard. Mr Hope was then summoned for permitting drunkenness on licensed premises. The magistrates told him that his daughter was too young to be left in charge and fined him 20*s*.[2]

No fixed address
1888

After closing up the *Coach & Horses* in Swinegate on the night of Thursday 3 May, landlord Thomas Barnacle looked out of his bedroom window and saw a woman lying in the street. He called to her to get up, warning her that the police would be coming, but she told him 'I can't'. He came downstairs and into the street as a policeman approached them and held his lantern over the woman. The light showed that her head was laid in a pool of blood. 'Silly old woman to get yourself in this state,' Thomas said to her and she replied 'I've had nothing, scarcely'. He helped the policeman walk a few yards with her and went back inside the *Coach & Horses*.

The inquest on her death was held there two days later. She was identified as sixty-year-old widow Maria Webster, of no fixed address.

Her head was laid in a pool of blood

The landlord said he had seen her a week before when she had been seeking lodgings but she had not been into the *Coach & Horses* on the night she was found lying in the street, nor had he seen her outside when he locked up. The surgeon reported that she had a scalp wound five inches long, and was cut to the bone, but she was suffering from no other injuries or a feeble constitution. A verdict of death while she was drunk was returned.[3]

Death of a hairdresser
1823

Towards the end of September a group of friends were holding a drinking party in the *Old White Swan* in Goodramgate. William Jackson, a hairdresser from a few doors away in Girdlegate (now Church Street), arrived to shave one of the gentlemen and while he was there they plied him with a great variety of drinks. William, described as being a person of weak mind and prone to liquor, eagerly continued to drink with them throughout the night. At about 7 o'clock the following morning he was carried unconscious from the inn and remained in that state for about six hours before a surgeon was sent for. The surgeon arrived but could not revive him, and within a few hours William had died.

At the inquest, held at the inn on the same day, it was revealed that at some time during the drinking session one of the party sent the

He was carried unconscious from the inn

waiter to buy 6*d* of tincture of jalap, a powdered root purgative, from a nearby druggist. It was strongly suspected that for a joke one of the men had mixed this with William's drinks but the surgeon gave his opinion that even if William had swallowed all of the jalap it could not have accelerated his death. A verdict was given of death by excessive drinking.[4]

The half-gallon jug
1863

At about 3 o'clock on a Tuesday afternoon in March, labourer Charles Precious from Walmgate went into the kitchen at the *Coach and Horses* in Nessgate, an inn we have already visited with two young chimney sweeps.

About half an hour later, John Goodricke, a farm labourer from Fulford, came in with a half-gallon jug of gin under his arm which he had bought from Mr Smith's in Friargate. He asked for a corkscrew and used it to open the jug, inviting everyone there to drink from it. Pouring some of the contents into a tumbler glass, he turned to Charles and asked if he would like a drink. Thinking it was water, Charles said he would prefer ale, but John persuaded him to drink it. It tasted good and Charles was easily persuaded to drink another tumbler-full.

Mary Ann McDonald, who worked as cook at the *Coach and Horses*, said that Charles then 'turned queer directly, kicked about and fell down'. Charles had seemed to be sober when he came in, and she asked John Goodricke what had been in the tumbler. He admitted that it was gin, and that he had bought it elsewhere and had taken it into the *Coach and Horses*. Amid the commotion, Mary Ann asked William Bentley, who worked as the boots, to take Charles outside, thinking he was going to be sick. William came into the room, and found Charles 'rolling about the long settee'. He took him outside and tried to support him, but Charles was too heavy for him to hold and fell into the gutter. William left him there and four policemen came along, picked him up, and carried him to the police station where he died that evening.

The inquest the next morning was in the *Exchange Hotel* in Church Street. John Goodricke said he had been too drunk to remember what happened. He recalled that a porter and a shoemaker had been present but said, 'I don't remember asking for a corkscrew. I carried the jug with me when I went away. It fell out of my arms in Castlegate and broke'. The verdict was death by congestion of the brain brought on by excessive drinking of gin.[5]

CHAPTER 18

Hard Times

Starved to death
1847

In the 1840s York's population rose 26 per cent to more than 36,000 compared with only 10 per cent the previous decade. The growth was due largely to the significant influx of Irish people who came to York as a result of the famines, which were particularly devastating in the west of the country. The warnings of 1822 and 1826 had gone largely unheeded and the partial failure of the potato crop in 1846 was followed by a complete failure the next year. By 1847 three million people in Ireland were dependent on nourishment from government soup kitchens. Within three years a million had died and another million left their homes to cross the Atlantic and the Irish Sea. Some fared little better when they arrived in England.

They came to escape the famines

On Wednesday afternoon of Thursday 27 April 1847 there was an inquest at William McLaren's *Burns Coffee House* on the body of a child aged two and a half who had died the previous night. The child and its parents were natives of Ireland and had arrived in York the previous evening by way of Leeds. There was a vagrant office in York at that time, offering lodgings for such people, but because of the great influx of Irish arriving daily to seek work as labourers it was full. The officers there placed the family in some lodgings in Jubbergate which had been set aside, but the child was already very ill and died the same night. The jury's verdict was that it died from the want of sufficient food and proper attention.

On Tuesday 26 January of that same year an inquest had been held at the Frog Hall in view of the body of thirty-year-old Mary Noble. It was said that her mother was in her seventies and had been in receipt of only 3s a week from the parish. Mary had been in poor health for some years and on the Thursday afternoon had been suddenly taken seriously ill and had died shortly afterwards in her chair. The jury were told that she had recently been suffering from an insufficiency of food and they reached a verdict that Mary had died from convulsions occasioned from the want of the proper necessities of life.[1]

A death in the vagrants' office
1824

In the days before the Irish famines, the hardship of the island's inhabitants was already being witnessed in York. On Wednesday 20 May there was an inquest at the *Globe Inn* in the Shambles on two-year-old Catherine Coffey, the child of two Irish tramps who had come to the city in search of employment. The previous night she had been taken by her parents to the vagrants' office seriously ill, and they watched over her until she died at midnight.[2]

Ready for the poor house
1829

On Tuesday 4 November there was an inquest at George Hutchinson's *Malt Shovel* in Walmgate on the body of Stephen Coleman who hanged himself that morning in his room. Stephen was in his seventies and had been very ill for some time. He believed the parish officials were planning to send him to the poor house and it was believed this had been very much preying on his mind. The jury returned a verdict of insanity.[3]

Perpendicular

For the past thirty years Thomas Eagle, landlord of *The Leopard* in Coppergate, had been acquainted with Robert Atkinson, better known to his friends as 'Perpendicular'. In the nineteenth century, customers who propped up the front bars of the city's inns getting steadily inebriated were known as perpendicular drinkers, but Robert's nickname seems to have been on account of his often being flat on his back. For the past three years he had lived in a single room down a passage near to the inn, in abject poverty brought on by his intemperance. Now aged sixty-four, he scraped an existence by running errands, being treated to drinks by his numerous friends. They knew him to be a well-educated man – he had been a valet for many gentlemen of distinction and had travelled in France, Spain and other places.

Robert now visited *The Leopard* almost every day, and on Christmas Day 1840 his friends bought him three small glasses of rum there and he wished Mr Eagle compliments of the season. Before 9 o'clock in the evening, he sat down in the kitchen of the inn and Mrs Eagle said to him 'You're very low spirited, what's the matter?' He replied he was very thirsty and had nothing to buy a drink with. She said 'Well I'll give you a pint of ale as it's Christmas time'. After that he had another glass, which he paid for out of his own pocket, then Mr Eagle took him home.

Two days later, on the Friday, Robert was back in *The Leopard* for four hours and he said he was much better but and when Mr Eagle offered him a drink he said he would just have ale. He did not come in on the Saturday, and on the Sunday he died in his room. The inquest was held in *The Leopard* at 8 o'clock on New Year's Eve, where the verdict was given that he died by the visitation of God.[4]

CHAPTER 19

An End to it All

A skeleton at the *White Swan*
1851

Isabella Lockwood had been landlady at the *White Swan* in Pavement since 1834, and had kept the business going on her own since her husband William died in 1842. Eight years later she also died and the inn closed for a time while it was being cleaned and repaired for the new landlord.

On Thursday 1 May, Robert Druggett, one of the workmen, was in a small windowless attic which adjoined the servants' sleeping quarters when he discovered a small paper box. He opened it and found, wrapped in old newspaper and towel, the skeleton of a child. He told his fellow workers, but nothing was done with the skeleton

The White Swan, *built as a coaching inn in 1733*

until the Wednesday of the following week when he was advised to report his discovery to the parish constable. It was found that the newspaper was a London daily containing the trial of Fergus O'Connor which had been held at the York Assizes ten or eleven years before. Mr Moore, the surgeon, said he was under the impression that the child had been born prematurely.[1]

A new-born child
1859

Beside the *Hand & Heart* in St Sampson's Square there ran a public passage known as Sweep Alley, connecting the square with Swinegate. The inn's water closet was accessed through this alley, and for a few days the lock had been broken. On a cold November morning, the landlady Mrs Lazenby was told that the basin was blocked. She took a pair of tongs and pulled out the body of a new-born baby boy wrapped in a black alpaca apron. She took the body into the *Hand & Heart*, washed it and reported her discovery to the police. The coroner saw that there was only one small mark of violence on the body below the right eye, but that the navel string had been broken about half a yard from the body and not tied and scarcely any blood

A passage known as Sweep Alley

was found internally. He concluded that, with proper care and attention, the child would have survived to be healthy and strong and adjourned the case so that the mother could be found. The following week there was still no clue as to the mother's identity and the jury returned a verdict that the child died from want of proper attention at the time of birth.[2]

A shocking discovery
1889

On 4 May, Fred Williamson and James Helstrip were out on a Sunday morning walk in Dringhouses. As they were going through the field on St Helen's Road next to the new railway bridge over the York-London line, Fred noticed a parcel lying partly-opened in the grass. He looked inside and found it contained the body of a child. It had been buried but dug up, probably by dogs, and the left arm and mangled head were almost torn away from the badly decomposed body. About 10 yards away, they found some newspaper covered in blood. James went to find a policeman and returned with sergeant William Humphries who had the parcel and its contents taken to *The Fox* on Tadcaster Road where the inquest was later held. The jury was told that the body was of a new-born baby girl, who had been born alive but had lived for no more than four days. There were grounds to believe that the mother had been given no medical attention, but her identity was never traced and the jury returned an open verdict.[3]

A deranged woman
1829

On Monday 10 November, shoemaker John Thompson rose from his bed at the *John Bull* in Layerthorpe at 7 o'clock in the morning. He seemed to be in good health, but as he opened the bedroom window he complained of feeling ill. He lay down on the bed and died almost immediately.

The inquest was held two days later at the *John Bull* when the usual verdict of the day, died by the visitation of God, was given. While the inquest was being heard, a woman called Elizabeth Feaster was also at the inn, in what the press reports described as a deranged state of mind. She was being attended to by people about to take her to the asylum, but she managed to escape from them, ran out of the inn and threw herself into the River Foss. Alfred Wilson, the landlord's son, raced after her and leapt into the river to rescue her. She was brought back to the *John Bull* but no sooner had she been changed into dry clothes than she escaped again but was caught by the landlord's daughter before she could throw herself back into the river. She was then taken to York Lunatic Asylum by the parish officers.[4]

Poisoning at the *Wheatsheaf*
1829

In August an inquest was held at the *Wheatsheaf* outside Walmgate bar, into the death of John Wales who had poisoned himself in the inn with arsenic. He had bought it saying he was going to use it as rat poison and when surgeon George Brown had been called to the inn John told him he had taken 2d worth of white mercury. Relatives said he had often talked of killing himself but never had the courage to do it. The verdict was that he took poison with the intention of alarming his parents so as to induce them into receiving him into his house and without the intention of destroying himself.[5]

Bad medicine at *The Clock*
1844

Jack Coultate, a twenty-seven-year-old groom, lived with his mother and his brother Henry in Black Bull passage off Walmgate. From about 12.30 on the afternoon before New Year's Eve he was drinking in the nearby *Clock* in the company of a woman called 'Tambourine Peg' and her husband, Thomas Quinn, 'Painter Sam', John Smith, Charles Emerson and some others.

At about 3 o'clock Emerson borrowed 3d to get something to eat and left the inn. He went to Mr Agar's druggist shop where he bought a pennyworth of laudanum, a medicine containing a tincture of opium. Mr Agar saw him put about 120 to 130 drops in a small ale glass and leave to go in the direction of *The Clock*. The druggist said later that twenty or thirty drops was the usual medicinal dose and that Emerson had bought laudanum from him on previous occasions. Emerson came back into *The Clock* and took a quart mug with some ale in it from where the group were drinking into another room. He brought it back and put it on the table and the company passed round the mug until it was empty.

John Smith, who had known Jack Coultate for six or seven years, left the inn at about 4 o'clock but returned an hour later. As he came in through the back door he found Jack laid on the floor with his head forward resting on his chest. He immediately pulled Jack's head clear and loosened his shirt neck and neckerchief. He asked 'Jack, are you badly?' but there was no answer. He said to the landlord, George Gibson, 'This is a dying man'. John asked the landlord to fetch medical help but the local surgeon Mr Mann was not at home so they sent for Mr Abbey. At about 5.30 a woman left the inn to go to tell

Jack's family. Jack's brother, Henry, arrived to find him on a seat under the window with his shoes off, his waistcoat open and his neckerchief dragged off his neck. He was leaning unconscious against the wall. Thinking his brother was very drunk, Henry tried to lift him, and someone helped him to get him home. Soon afterwards Mr Abbey arrived there, but was unable to help.

Meanwhile Henry had returned to *The Clock* where he heard that Jack had taken laudanum. He found Charles Emerson there and asked him 'Have you fetched any laudanum from Mr Agar's?' Emerson replied 'No, I haven't, I'll swear I haven't, upon my soul I haven't', and left the inn. Henry followed him and taking hold of his arm said 'I'll have the police fetched'. Emerson raised his arm as if threatening to strike Henry, who left him and went home to find that his brother had died at about 6 o'clock.

Mrs Coultate had taken ill with shock at her son's death, and she died at about 7.30. Half an hour later, Inspector Bellerby went to Emerson's house, found him in bed, and immediately took him into custody. The inquest was held that same night at Thomas Loy's *Black Bull* a few doors away amidst great excitement but there were no witnesses to say that John Coultate had drunk from the glass.[6]

A body in the *White Horse* stables
1850

In July, thirty-six-year-old William Tontill, a farmer from Birkin near Ferrybridge, was visiting York to attend the assizes. He was a witness at the forgery trial of his brother-in-law from Hull. On the Wednesday afternoon he went to the *Windmill*, an old inn on the riverbank close to the castle and law courts, accompanied by Sergeant Hobson of the Hull police. They each had a soda, which the sergeant paid for, and Thomas said he was so worried about the case that he had not slept at night since the trial began.

The following day he was missing and at 1 o'clock in the afternoon one of his friends, a Mr Kirby, called at the *White Horse* in Coppergate to look for him. James Stodhart, the ostler, helped him search and eventually they found him in a stall in the stables. The stall was dark and had no straw in it, and they saw William lying on the bare floor. Thinking that he had taken more than enough drink and was sleeping it off, they quietly left, closing the stable door so that no-one would disturb him. Half an hour later William's brother Joseph arrived and the ostler took him into the stable where William was still lying in exactly the same position. The ostler went to fetch a candle and in the dim light they saw blood glistening on the floor and a knife lying close by. Joseph sent for Dr North who found two wounds in William's

One of his friends called at the White Horse

neck. The one on the left side was not deep, but the wound on the right had cut an artery and it was clear that William was dead. There was commotion out in the street when passers-by discovered what had happened.

At the inquest Mr Mitchell said that William had called into his shop in Stonegate at 11 o'clock the day he died and bought the knife. At the time he had seemed to be in a jocular mood and had spent five minutes sharpening the knife before he left the shop to go to the *White Horse*. The coroner was critical of William's friends for failing to keep a close watch on him, but magistrate Coleman pointed out that William had deliberately slipped away from their company. The jury gave a verdict that William had destroyed himself while he was in a state of unsound mind.[7]

The icy hand of death
1838

On Friday evening 12 October at the *Black Horse* in Pavement an inquest was held in view of the body of William Ingles. William, a Scot, was over seventy but still worked as a drover for some sheep dealers based in his native land, and would have often made the journey south with his flocks. Two days before, he had been at the cattle market where sheep were also traded, and returned to the *Black Horse* where he was lodging, complaining of feeling ill. Surgeon Brown was called to attend him, and in the meantime his employers also visited the inn to pay him the three sovereigns he had earned for his long journey. They advised him to rest there.

At 6 o'clock on the Friday morning he was served with coffee but asked for tea instead. The local press reported that by the time the servant had returned with his tea she found, it was reported, that 'the icy hand of death' had finished the old drover's earthly career. The coroner's jury gave the usual verdict for death by natural causes – died suddenly by the visitation of God.[8]

Leeches on the brain
1827

Eleven years earlier another drover John Campbell was returning home from Norwich, passing through York with his cattle. On Friday evening 3 November he stayed at the *Black Horse* in Bootham, and

He applied leeches to the drover's head

was found in his bed at 6 o'clock the following morning very ill and in a complete state of stupor. Landlord Joseph Leetall and his family did what they could for him and a surgeon was called who applied leeches to the drover's head, but with no success, and he died at about noon. His head was opened by surgeons who found an effusion in the left ventricle of the brain, which they believed was the cause of death.[9]

A lodger at the *Black Horse*
1888

On Saturday 9 June William Mason, landlord of the *Black Horse* in Walmgate, was called upon to attend an inquest at *The Saddle* in Fulford. The previous day the body of an unknown man had been found in the river at Fulford. He had been seen at lunchtime on the Thursday, talking to another man about agriculture and generally passing the time and it seems that someone had a clue to his identity.

William identified the body as that of Joseph Bannister, who had been lodging at the *Black Horse* for the past two months. He was from Nottingham and the landlord believed him to have been a horse dealer and aged about sixty-four. Soon after he had arrived at the *Black Horse* one of Joseph's sons came on horseback to visit him, but he stayed only a couple of nights and there had been no more visitors since.

A fellow horse-dealer, William Holliday of Navigation Road, said that Joseph had once kept a lodging house in Nottingham but no longer did anything, but was always quite lively. He was a widower and would often speak of his wife. He said the last time he saw Joseph had been in the *Black Horse* where he had drunk 2d worth of wine. The landlord said that the last time he saw Joseph was before he went to bed on the Tuesday at about 11 o'clock. By the time he came downstairs the next morning Joseph had already eaten breakfast and left. The landlord added that Joseph always appeared to be in the best of spirits and paid his bills on time. He was not a betting man but sometimes placed a shilling or two on the horses. He had once had a very good watch but Mr Mason had not seen it lately. All Joseph left behind was a watch chain, knife and ring. There were no marks on his body and a verdict of suicide was returned but there was not sufficient evidence to show his state of mind.[10]

A loose life
1881

On Wednesday 14 October, thirty-one-year-old Edwin Fox visited Copmanthorpe village where until a few weeks before he had worked in a chemist's shop. He had moved out of the village because of a family quarrel and no longer worked. For the past three weeks he had been staying at the appropriately named *Fox Inn* in Petergate and was said to have been living a loose life in York and in Scarborough.

On that Wednesday he arrived back at the *Fox* at 10 o'clock in the evening and went to bed at 11.30. He did not rise at the usual time and at about noon a young man named Dalby was sent to find him. The young man found Edwin in his bedroom in an unconscious state and immediately called for help, but Edwin died before it arrived. In his room was found a bottle containing some salts of prussic acid. This, and scars on his neck from a previous attempt on his own life, led the coroner to a verdict of suicide.[11]

A cut-throat razor
1843

Five years later, a commercial traveller by the name of Bower was staying at the *Golden Fleece*, then more usually known simply as the *Fleece*, in Pavement. He was in town for the July assizes where he was due to appear as a plaintiff in a case concerning wages and slept at the inn, sharing a room with two other guests. At about 1 o'clock in the morning one of the guests heard a moan and lit a candle to see what had happened. He found that Mr Bower had cut his throat just under his chin and was bleeding heavily, with a razor lying beside him. Remarkably, given the time of night, three surgeons arrived to treat him and found that he had missed his windpipe and major blood vessels. It was later reported that he was occasionally delirious, but hopes of his recovery were high.[12]

An inspector of cruelty
1889

Thomas Pumphrey, an inspector of cruelty to children, went into the *Waggon & Horses* in Gillygate on the morning of Thursday 16 May and asked the landlord Thomas Thompson for a room, as he felt tired. The landlord showed him to a room where the inspector lay down on a sofa. He served him several times during the day, and Mr Pumphrey seemed to be in good health, but in the afternoon he was still complaining of feeling ill and asked if he could stay a little longer. 'Are you going to have a drink with me?' he asked the landlord. Mr Thompson replied 'I don't mind having something with you' and went to get one for himself. When Mr Pumphrey handed over the money to pay for the drinks the landlord noticed some blood on his hands and asked him about it. 'I've scratched a spot off my face' he joked, but the landlord saw more blood on his face and asked him if he had been injuring himself. He replied 'Not that I know of', but the

He went into the Waggon and Horses

landlord then noticed a jagged wound on his neck and asked him if he needed any help. He answered that he did and the landlord took him to the County hospital. The wound was found to be two inches in length and half an inch deep and was in a very dangerous place and the defendant was detained in hospital until Wednesday last on account of delirium.

A week later Mr Pumphrey was charged with having attempted suicide by cutting his own throat with a knife. His defence said that it was a case of disappointed love and Mr Pumphrey had been on the eve of being married when the lady broke off the engagement. This, coupled with his mother's illness, was more than he could bear. He was kept in custody until someone could be found to take care of him, and a week later it was reported that his brother had come forward to take him.[13]

Incident at *Jacob's Well*
1838

The *Jacob's Well* still stands in Trinity Lane off Micklegate. Named after the spring where Christ asked a Samaritan woman for a drink, for the greater part of its life the house has had religious connections, but during most of the nineteenth century it was appropriately a public house, fulfilling one of the corporal works of mercy by supplying drinks to the thirsty.

On Sunday evening 13 May a man named Feasby was quietly sitting here when shocked customers saw him take a knife from his pocket and attempt to cut his throat. They immediately caught hold of him and prevented his suicide, although his hands were badly cut in the struggle. The press reported that the incident had caused a great sensation in the neighbourhood, but the man had now been delivered into the safe custody of his friends.[14]

Murder at the *Queen's Head*
1864

Irishman Thomas Palfreman was a wheelwright for the North Eastern Railway Company. On the evening of Saturday 21 May he went into the *Queen's Head* in Fossgate and 'started to chaff in Irish'. He walked up to a table where four labourers were sitting and probably desperate for beer money he offered to fight any one of them for a shilling. One of the men, John Walker, had a pipe and tobacco in his hand and, telling the Irishman he wanted no trouble, he stood up to get a light. As he rose, Palfreman struck him in the face and, as Walker fell, Palfreman kicked him in the ribs. Walker said he was blinded with blood and remembered nothing more. It seems that another of the four, thirty-six-year-old John Foy, then struck Palfreman in the face, Palfreman struck back and a general free-for-all followed. Suddenly Palfreman clutched his stomach and cried 'I'm stabbed!' The police arrived and arrested everyone in the inn, but knives were found on only two of them and both knives were too small to have caused the wound.

On the Sunday morning a charwoman found a bloodstained knife in the kitchen where the stabbing had taken place. It had a long blade and a spring in the back to stop it closing. On the Monday Thomas Palfreman died of his injuries. John Foy was found guilty of manslaughter and given twenty years' penal servitude.[15]

Miscellaneous Notes

Pre-decimal currency in Britain was:

4 farthings = 1 penny (1*d*);
12 pence = 1 shilling (1*s*), equivalent to the modern 5p;
2*s* 6*d* = half a crown;
20 shillings = 1 pound (£1); and
21 shillings = 1 guinea.

Usually low pound values were expressed in shillings, e.g. 20*s* instead of £1, as payment would normally be made in coinage.

After inflation caused by the Napoleonic Wars, prices fell by about one-third towards the middle of the nineteenth century, and had risen again by 12 per cent in 1900.

Typical prices at the end of the century were 1*d* for a pint of cheap watered beer or a pound of flour, 2½*d* for a dozen eggs, and 5*d* for a pound of beef.

Casual labourers might be paid 3*s* or 4*s* for a 10-hour 6-day week and a painter or bricklayer would be paid about 6*s* 6*d*. A maid's wages might start at 5*s* a week, with a groom being paid about twice that amount, the same as a coach guard who would also receive tips. A butler would typically be paid £1 a week, and the £3 a week middle-class earnings would have seemed like a fortune to most people.

Drinks were served in measures of 8 gills = 2 pints = 1 quart.

Bibliography

The Army in York 1750–1800 – W B Taylor, 1991.

Brewster session records.

Census returns 1841–1891.

A Directory of York Pubs 1455–2003 – Hugh Murray, 2004.

Family Herald.

Feeding a City – Eileen White, 2000.

Life in Regency York – Prudence Bebb, 1992.

The Medieval Markets and Fairs of York – H Richardson, 1961.

The New Guide for Strangers and Residents in the City of York 1838.

The Old Inns and Inn Signs of York – T P Cooper, 1897.

Parish registers.

Poverty, a Study of Town Life – B Seerbohm Rowntree, 1901.

Poverty & Prejudice, A Study of Irish Immigrants in York -- Frances Finnegan, 1982.

Poverty & Prostitution -- Frances Finnegan, 1989.

York Castle records of deliveries and sentences.

York Chronicle.

York Courant.

York Gazette.

York Herald.

York – Its Markets and Fairs – George Benson, 1932.

York Register of Alehouses.

York – Royal Commission on Historical Monuments, 1981.

Yorkshire Evening Press.

Yorkshireman.

Various street and trade directories.

References to Publications

Key: FH = *Family Herald*; YCh = *York Chronicle*; YCo = *York Courant*;
YG = *York Gazette*; YH = *York Herald*; Ym = *The Yorkshireman*.

Introduction
[1] YH 10 Jan 1857.

Chapter 1
[1] YH 20, 27 Feb, 5, 12, 19 March 1808, [2] YCo 26 March, 23 April, 19 Nov 1822, 13 May 1823, [3] YH 2 May 1829 , [4] YH 26 June, 7 July 1838, [5] YH 20 April 1899.

Chapter 2
[1] YH 25 Jan 1800, [2] YH 6 Oct 1849, [3] YH 30 Nov 1850, [4] YH 20 Aug 1825, [5] YH 17 Sept 1842, [6] YH 28 Sept 1850, [7] YCo 1 Oct 1840.

Chapter 3
[1] YH 30 March 1861, [2] YH 29 June 1844, [3] YH 5, 12 Sept 1885, [4] YH 27 July 1829, [5] YH 11 July 1854, [6] YH 8 July 1843, [7] YG 26 Feb 1848, [8] YH 8 Oct 1853, [9] YH 27 Nov 1852, 8 Jan 1853, [10] YH 19 Aug 1837, [11] YH 1 Aug 1857, [12] YH 8, 15 Jan 1870, [13] YH 22 June 1816, [14] YH 11 April 1829, [15] YH 2 Nov 1850, [16] YH 23 Aug 1873, [17] YH 12 Sept 1829, [18] YH 5, 12 May 1888, [19] YH 2 Sept 1865.

Chapter 4
[1] YH 7 Sept 1850, [2] YH 7 May 1864, [3] YH 8 March 1873, [4] YH 8 Oct 1859, [5] YH 9 Feb 1839, [6] YG 2 Jan 1847, [7] YH 15 Aug 1857, [8] YCo 2 July 1822, [9] YG 10 July 1847, [10] YH 5 Nov 1842, [11] YH 14, 21 April 1804, [12] YH 14 Oct 1820, [13] YCh 21 July 1831, [14] YH 12, 30 Jan 1836, [15] YH 15 Feb 1851, [16] YH 12 Feb 1853, [17] YH 29 Aug 1863, [18] YH 3 Nov 1866, [19] YCo 28 May 1840.

Chapter 5
[1] YH 9 Sept 1854, [2] YH 15 Aug 1863, [3] YH 18 Feb 1843, [4] FH Feb 1858, [5] YH 14 June 1851.

Chapter 6
[1] YH 31 Aug 1872, [2] YH 1 Jan 1803, [3] YCh 3 Sept 1812, [4] YH 5 March 1803, [5] YH 1 May 1864, [6] YH 6 May 1854, 20 April, 15 June 1889, [7] YH 1 March 1851, [8] YH 25 March 1863, [9] YH 14 March 1874, 10 March 1888, [10] YH 17 Oct 1874, [11] YH 29 Jan, 5 Feb 1887.

Chapter 7

[1]YH 10 Dec 1825, [2]YH 22 June 1839, [3]YH 19 Sept 1852, [4]YH 10 Nov 1855, [5]YH 27 March 1858, 9 June, 8 Sept 1860, Jan 1861, 12 Dec 1863, [6]YCo and YH 21 Dec 1822, YG 26 Oct 1833, Ym 23 March 1833, 27 Sept 1834, YG 2 July 1853, YH 8 Jan, 24 April 1859, [7]YH 17 March, 3 July 1858, 3, 16 July 1859. 3 Jan 1862, 6 Feb 1869, 29 Oct 1875, 30 Oct 1880, [8]YH 22 Feb, 17 May, 9 Aug 1873.

Chapter 8

[1]YH 12 April 1851, [2]YH 1 June 1889, [3]YH 5 Feb 1881, [4]YH 8 June 1844, [5]YCh 6 March, 17 April 1834, [6]YH 26 Feb 1842.

Chapter 9

[1]YH 16 Aug 1851, [2]YG 13 Feb 1847, [3]YH 5 Oct 1873, [4]YH 11 Aug 1838, [5]Ym 18 Sept 1852, [6]YH 18 May 1889.

Chapter 10

[1]YH 15 April 1809, [2]YH 12 July 1851, 14 May 1853, 30 July 1853, etc., [3]YH 11 Oct 1851, 31 Aug 1861, 31 Oct 1863, 2 Jan, 23 Jan 19 Mar, 16 July 1864, [4]YH 18 May 1850, 2 Oct, 24 Nov 1852, [5]YH 5 March 1836, [6]YG 16 Dec 1848, [7]YH 27 Nov 1880, [8]YH 29 Aug 1863, [9]YH 30 July, 6 Aug 1864, [10]YH 27 April, 18, 25 May 1850, [11]YH 1, 18 July 1874, [12]*Yorkshire Evening Press* 23 January 1896.

Chapter 11

[1]YH 10 Feb 1866, [2]YCh 10 Jan 1833, [3]YH 28 Jan 1855, [4]YH 27 Oct 1855, [5]YH 31 Oct 1857, [6]YH 30 Jan, 29 March, 10 April 1858, [7]YH 12 Aug 1843, 20 April 1844, [8]YH 17 Nov 1849, 3, 10 May 1851, [9]YH 1 Nov 1851, 10 April 1852, 6 Oct 1855, 4 April 1857, [10]YH 30 Aug 1851, 6 May 1854, 12 Feb 1857 etc., [11]YH 3, 8 April, 8 May 1858, [12]YG 27 Feb 1847, YH 2 Feb 1850, 16 Jan 1858, 6 Jan 1860, etc. Frances Finnegan – *Poverty and Prostitution in York*, 1979, [13]YH 31 Dec 1842, 18 Oct 1873 etc., [14]YH 29 July 1854, 26 Feb, 9 April 1859, 5 Jan 1861, 17, 24 March, 22 Oct 1866.

Chapter 12

[1]YH 21 Nov 1829, York Spring Assizes 1833, [2]YH 7 Oct 1820, [3]YH 19 Jan 1839, [4]YH 30 Oct 1824, [5]YCo 25 Jan 1825, [6]YCh 17 May, 27 Dec 1827, [7]YH 26 April, 15, 22 Aug, 21 Nov 1829, [8]YH 2 Jan, 5 March 1836, [9]YH 24 Feb 1838, [10]YH 21 July, 28 July, 11 Aug 1838, [11]YH 20 July 1839, [12]YH 28 Sept, 5 Oct 1861, [13]YCo 3 April 1877, [14]YH 21 July 1877.

Chapter 13

[1]YH 13 April, 11 May, 20 July 1839, [2]YH 29 May 1824, [3]YH 29 Aug 1885, [4]YH 18 May, 25 May 1880.

Chapter 14

[1]YCh 6 Jan 1831, [2]YH 9 Jan 1830, [3]YH 2 Jan 1874, [4]YH 18 Dec 1880, [5]YCo 3 Jan 1801.

Chapter 15

[1]YH 27 April 1816, [2]YH 21 Jan 1843, [3]YH 27 May 1854, [4]YH 13 Nov 1858, [5]YH 3 Feb 1845, [6]YH 20 April 1850, [7]YH 12 Jan 1855, [8]YH 1 Jan 1859, [9]YCh 7 April 1831, [10]YH 13 Jan 1866, [11]YH 27 March 1858, [12]YH 11 Jan 1852, 10 Nov 1860, [13]YH 13 Feb 1858, [14]YH 13 March 1858, [15]YH 30 Jan 1869, [16]YH 8 Jan 1848.

Chapter 16

[1]YH 17 Feb 1810, [2]YH 28 Dec 1850, [3]YG 5 Jan, YCh 10, 24 April 1833, [4]YH 22 Feb 1868, [5]YCo 23 July 1840, [6]YH 18 June 1840, [7]YH 19 April, 13 Sept 1851, [8]YH 7 July 1866, [9]YH 26 April, 2 July 1851, [10]YH 25 April, 12 June, 18 July 1863, [11]YH 29 Nov 1851, [12]YH 9 May 1863, [13]YH 28 Nov 1863, [14]YH 5 Dec 1863, YH 1, 8 May 1864, [16]YH 4 Jan 1868, [17]YH 25 Jan 1868.

Chapter 17

[1]YH 25 Aug, 1 Sept 1855, [2]YH 1 April 1887, [3]YH 26 May 1888, [4]YCo 30 Sept 1823, [5]YH 28 March 1863.

Chapter 18

[1]YG 30 Jan, 1 May 1847, [2]YH 22 May 1824, [3]YH 7 Nov 1829, [4]YH 4 Jan 1841.

Chapter 19

[1]YH 10 May 1851, [2]YH 26 Nov, 3 Dec 1859, [3]YH 11 May 1889, [4]YH 14 Nov 1829, [5]YH 29 Aug 1829, [6]YH 31 Dec 1844, [7]YH 20 July 1850, [8]YG 13 Oct 1838, [9]YCh 8 Nov 1827, [10]YH 9 June 1888, [11]YH 15, 22 Oct 1881, [12]YH 22 July 1843, [13]YH 8, 13 June 1889, [14]YH 19 May 1838, [15]YH 6 Aug 1864.

Disclaimer: commentary as to guilt or innocence of any person mentioned in this book is based on contemporary reports and does not necessarily reflect the author's opinion.

Index

People

Abbey, surgeon 43, 52, 153
Agar, druggist 153
Allen, surgeon 7, 38
Alp, policeman 58, 70, 87
Andrews, John 16
Anson, William 33
Antonio, Joseph 7
Appleton, George 61
Armitage, William 30
Arnott, ostler 16
Atkinson, Robert 148
Atkinson, sergeant 130
Atkinson, Thomas 21, 77
Austick, John 127

Bagley, policeman 92
Bainbridge, policeman 62, 70
Baines, George 127
Baird, surgeon 33
Ball, Alfred 24
Bannister, Joseph 157
Barber, James 43
Barker, Oswald 136
Barnacle, Thomas 144
Barrett, Benjamin 59
Bates, Samuel 93
Battle, Anthony 139
Battle, John 139
Beal, policeman 68
Bean, Christopher 8
Beaumont, Elizabeth 104
Beaumont, John 81
Beaumont, waiter 113
Belcombe, doctor 34
Bellerby, policeman 97
Bendigo, boxer 118
Benson, glass retailer 111
Benson, J, coach proprietor 106
Bentley, William 146
Berry, landlord 77
Bethany, Alfred 93
Bew, soldier 129
Bewley, tobacconist 115
Birbeck, Margaret 28
Birch, Bob 24
Blackburne, policeman 70
Blain, Ann 24

Blain, landlady 24
Blain, William 24
Bland, William 82
Blaney, sergeant 129
Blessington, Sarah Ann 71
Boland, Michael 85
Boltby, magistrate 143
Bond, Daniel 131
Booth, James 116
Boruwlaski, Joseph 57
Bower, commercial traveller 158
Bowser, Ann 135
Bowyer, Mrs 82
Boyne, Patrick 74
Bradley, Mrs 38
Braithwaite, Abraham 31
Braithwaite, landlady 31
Braithwaite, William 82
Brennan, James 140
Brennan, Michael 139
Briggs, Jane 80
Briggs, William 65
Broadmead, landlord 132
Brogan, Michael 140
Brown, Caroline 38
Brown, George 153
Brown, John 29, 57, 86
Brown, landlady 29
Brown, Leonard 133
Brown, Luke 116
Brown, Mr 11
Brown, policeman 73
Brown, shopkeeper 115
Brown, surgeon 156
Brownlee, James 69
Bruce, preacher 104
Buck, Margaret 101
Burke, boxer 118
Burke, William 89
Burr, saddler 129
Buttery, John 88

Caffrey, Anthony 137
Calvert, Annie 36
Calvert, Robert 36
Cameron, Robert 128
Campbell, John 156
Carney, Edward 103
Carney, Henry 143
Carr, Henry 30

Inns